A TRAVELER'S GUIDE TO CHINESE HISTORY

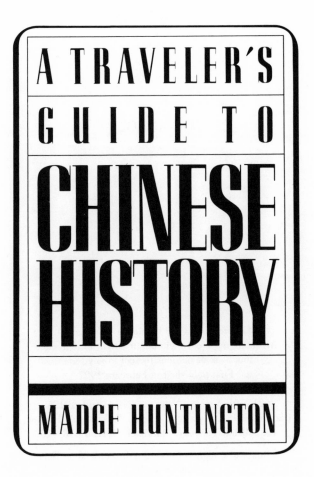

A TRAVELER'S GUIDE TO CHINESE HISTORY

MADGE HUNTINGTON

An Owl Book
Henry Holt and Company
New York

FOR ARNOLD

First published in February 1987
by Henry Holt and Company, Inc.,
521 Fifth Avenue, New York, New York 10175.
Distributed in Canada by Fitzhenry & Whiteside Limited,
195 Allstate Parkway, Markham, Ontario L3R 4T8.

Library of Congress Cataloging in Publication Data
Huntington, Madge.
A traveler's guide to Chinese history.
"An Owl book."
Bibliography: p.
Includes index.
1. China—History.   I. Title.
DS735.H84   1987   951   86–4767
ISBN 0-8050-0097–6 (pbk.)

First Edition

Designed by Lucy Albanese
Printed in the United States of America
1 3 5 7 9 10 8 6 4 2

ISBN 0-8050-0097-6

*Grateful acknowledgment is made to the following for permission to
reprint previously published material:*

Alfred A. Knopf, Inc., and Allen & Unwin for "The Autumn Wind," by Wu Ti, and
"The Ruins of Loyang," by Cao Zhi, from *Translations from the Chinese*, by Arthur
Waley, copyright © 1919 (copyright renewed 1947) by Arthur Waley.

China Institute in America for drawing of Qin palace (Figure 15), from *Chinese Traditional Architecture*, copyright © 1984 by Nancy Shatzman Steinhardt, p. 67; for plan
of Beijing (Figure 41), ibid., p. 143.

Columbia University Press for "Duckweed Pond," by Wang Wei, and "Autumn Cove,"
by Li Bai, both translated by Burton Watson, from *The Columbia Book of Chinese Poetry*,
copyright © 1984 by Columbia University Press.

Penguin Books Ltd. for extracts from *Marco Polo: The Travels* (Penguin Classics, 1958),
translated by Ronald Latham, copyright © 1958 by Ronald Latham, pp. 108, 133, 213,
214, 215–216.

Phoenix Art Museum for painting (Figure 31) by Yuan Yao (active 1720–1780), from
Chenxiang Pavilion (Leaf C from album of 12 leaves); d. 1740, ink and color on silk,
H. 35 cm, W. 41 cm, Accession no. 85/18.

Yale University Press for "Yearning," by Li Bai, translated by Stephen Owen, from *The
Great Age of Chinese Poetry*, copyright © 1981 by Yale University Press.

Figures 2, 4, 8, 10, 20, 25, 27, 32, 34, 37, 39, 40, and 46, painted in color on silk
by the Qing dynasty court painter Yao Wenhan (active 1760–1790), are from an album
called *Twenty-four Portraits of Chinese Emperors*.

CONTENTS

LIST OF MAPS

ACKNOWLEDGMENTS

I wish to express the profoundest gratitude to Professor S. T. Phen of Fudan University, Shanghai, whose expertise in Chinese history was generously shared at every step in the writing of this book. He directed me toward the best English-language sources for Chinese history, enriched my understanding of these with his own scholarly readings of Chinese-language sources, painstakingly read several drafts of the book, and helped clarify confusions where they arose. Throughout, his courteous and enthusiastic attention gave me a special understanding of the high standards and fine style of Chinese scholarship.

PREFACE

Before, during, and after a trip to China in 1984, I looked for a book which would tell me who the major figures in Chinese civilization were, figures who would stand out as mnemonic guides to their respective eras and whose stories would help hold an immensely complicated history in place. The book I looked for was not to be found, so, in the process of educating myself, I've ended up writing it.

In a civilization with a history covering over four thousand years, there are an enormous number of significant persons. For the sake of clarity, I've selected forty-five. The first is the mythical Bangu, a sort of God and Adam rolled into one. The next seven, also nonhistorical, are taken from a large group of legendary figures who appear in traditional accounts of Chinese history. Recorded history began during the Shang dynasty, c 1600–c 1100 B.C., and from this point on, the account is of real people who have had major roles in Chinese history and culture. Their stories are set into a very general historical outline with more particular accounts of events of the nineteenth and twentieth centuries. Appendixes on geography, art, and places to visit fill out this very abbreviated presentation of a vast subject.

Let me emphasize that the book is intended as an easily remembered overview, an initial guide to China's past for today's traveler. The more complete picture will build up little by little as the reader ventures into the vast literature available. A recommended reading list at the end of the book will help point the way.

GUIDE TO SPELLING, PRONUNCIATION, AND DATES

Spelling

The pinyin system devised by the People's Republic of China for the romanization of Chinese names is used throughout this book with the exceptions listed below. However, since many English texts both past and present still use the Wade-Giles system devised by non-Chinese in the nineteenth century, I have provided the Wade-Giles spelling, when it differs significantly from the pinyin, in brackets in the text and in the index. This may help reduce confusion should the reader wish to consult other histories as well.

Translations of names are placed in quotation marks in parenthesis.

Examples:

Pinyin	Wade-Giles	English
Bangu	[Pan-ku]	
Luoyang	[Lo-yang]	("North of the River Lo")

Exceptions:
The spelling of the following Chinese names is neither pinyin nor Wade-Giles but is used here because these forms are either familiar

xiii

or conventional in the West: Chiang Kai-shek, Confucius, I-ching, Manchukuo, Mencius, Soong Ching-ling, Soong Mei-ling, and Sun Yat-sen. In addition, some Chinese place names are better known by a conventional spelling than by their pinyin and/or Wade-Giles forms: Hong Kong, Canton (Guangzhou), Yangtse River, etc. Most of these conventional spellings can be found in the index, listed separately or after their pinyin and Wade-Giles forms. Some conventional spellings also appear in appendix III: Places to Visit.

Pronunciation

Pinyin words are pronounced more or less according to the rules of English phonetics. There are four significant exceptions:

C: *C* followed by vowel(s) is pronounced "ts," as in *its*; thus *Cao Cao* becomes "Tsao Tsao."

OU: *OU* rhymes with *oe* in *hoe*. *Zhou*, as in *Zhou dynasty*, becomes "joe."

Q: *Q* is pronounced "ch" as in *chin*. Thus *Qin* and *Qing* (dynasties) become "chin" and "ching," respectively.

X: *X* is spoken like a lisped *s*—also described as an aspirated *s*, or *hs*. *Xi'an* becomes "Hsi-ahn."

Dates

It is not possible to give accurate dates for events occurring in China prior to 841 B.C. Before the mid-twentieth century, Chinese historians had a tradition of attributing exact dates to the reigns of legendary rulers of the third millennium B.C. as well as to those of the historical Shang and Western Zhou dynasties in the first two millennia B.C. Modern archeological findings, based on carbon dating, do not confirm these early dates but replace them with slightly later approximated dates. The year 841 B.C. is significant because from then on, annual records, or annals, were kept which can be verified by a combination of archeological and astronomical data. The dates given in this text are those used by the China Institute in America.

CHINESE CHRONOLOGY

Date	Dynasty or Political Unit	Ruler or Major Figure
legend third millennium B.C.		Bangu Fuxi and Nuwa Shen Nong Huangdi Yao Shun
c 2100–c 1600	Xia (legendary)	Yu Jie
c 1600–c 1100	Shang (historical)	Tang Zhouxin
c 1100–771	Western Zhou	Zhou Wuwang Dan, Duke of Zhou You
770–221	Eastern Zhou	
770–476	Spring and Autumn period	Laozi Confucius
475–221	Warring States period	Mencius Shang Yang
221–207	Qin	Qin Shihuangdi

Date	Dynasty or Political Unit	Ruler or Major Figure
206 (B.C.)–8 A.D.	Western Han	Han Gaozu Han Wudi
9–23	Xin	Wang Mang
25–220	Eastern Han	Ban Chao Ban Zhao
220–265	Three Kingdoms	Zhugeliang
265–316	Western Jin	
317–589	Northern and Southern Dynasties	Bodhidharma
581–618	Sui	Sui Wendi Sui Yangdi
618–907	Tang	Tang Taizong Empress Wu Tang Xuanzong Li Bai
907–960	Five Dynasties, Ten Kingdoms	
960–1127	Northern Song	Song Taizu Wang Anshi Song Huizong
1127–1279	Southern Song	
1271–1368	Yuan (Mongol)	Kublai Khan Marco Polo
1368–1644	Ming	Ming Taizu The Yongle emperor Zheng He
1644–1911	Qing	The Kangxi emperor Cixi
1911–1949	Warlord Era, Republic of China	Sun Yat-sen Chiang Kai-shek
1949	People's Republic of China	Mao Zedong

PARALLEL CHRONOLOGY:
CHINA AND THE WEST

Date	Major Chinese Events	Major Chinese Figures	Western Events and Figures
4000 B.C.	Yangshao culture	Bangu	Sumerian culture, Mesopotamia
3000	Longshan culture	Fuxi and Nuwa Huangdi Shen Nong Yao Shun	Egyptian dynastic era begins First pyramids in Egypt
2000	Xia dynasty	Yu	Stonehenge begun in Great Britain
1800			Bronze Age; Abraham, Hammurabi
1700			Minoan Palace, Knossos,
		Jie	Crete

Date	Major Chinese Events	Major Chinese Figures	Western Events and Figures
1600	Shang dynasty Bronze Age, oracle bones, silk weaving	Tang	Mycenean era, Greece
1400			Tutankhamen rules in Egypt
1300			Trojan War
1200			Moses, exodus of Jews from Egypt
		Zhouxin	
1100	Western Zhou dynasty	Wuwang Duke of Zhou	
1000			King David makes Jerusalem his capital
900			Solomon builds Temple
800	Eastern Zhou dynasty Spring and Autumn period	You	Founding of Rome
700			Homer
600			Zoroaster
		Laozi	Buddha
		Confucius	Socrates
500	Warring States Period		Plato
400			Aristotle
300		Mencius	Alexander the Great
		Shang Yang	
	Qin dynasty	Qin Shihuangdi	Hannibal
200	Han dynasty	Han Gaozu Han Wudi	

Date	Major Chinese Events	Major Chinese Figures	Western Events and Figures
100 B.C.	Expansion into Central Asia	Sima Qian	Julius Caesar, Roman Empire
A.D.	Xin dynasty	Wang Mang	Jesus Christ
	Eastern Han dynasty	Ban Chao Ban Zhao	Nero
100	Paper invented		
200	Three Kingdoms	Zhugeliang	
300	Western Jin dynasty Northern and Southern Dynasties		Constantine
400			Attila the Hun invades Gaul
500			Fall of Rome Silk worms in Europe
	Sui dynasty	Sui Wendi	
600	Grand Canal	Sui Yangdi	Mohammed
	Tang dynasty	Tang Taizong	
700	Trade route restored Porcelain	Tang Xuanzong Li Bai	Dome of the Rock built in Jerusalem
800	Printing		Charlemagne
900	Gunpowder Five Dynasties, Ten Kingdoms Northern Song dynasty	Song Taizu	
1000		Wang Anshi	William the Conqueror
1100	Southern Song dynasty	Song Huizong Genghis Khan	Richard the Lion-Hearted; Third Crusade

Date	Major Chinese Events	Major Chinese Figures	Western Events and Figures
1200	Yuan dynasty (Mongol Empire)	Kublai Khan Marco Polo	Saint Francis of Assisi Chartres
1300	Ming dynasty	Ming Taizu	Dante
1400		The Yongle emperor Zheng He	Henry V in England
			Printing in Europe
			Columbus
1500	Portuguese at Macao		Magellan
			Shakespeare
1600	Qing dynasty (Manchu)	The Kangxi emperor	Louis XIV English and Dutch East India Companies founded
1700	Westerners trade at Guangzhou		Mozart American and French revolutions
1800	Opium Wars		Napoleon Queen Victoria
	Taiping Rebellion	Cixi	American Civil War
	Boxer Rebellion	Sun Yat-sen	Industrial Revolution
1900	Republic of China	Chiang Kai-shek	World War I Treaty of Versailles
	Japanese invasion	Mao Zedong	Depression World War II

Date	Major Chinese Events	Major Chinese Figures	Western Events and Figures
	People's Republic of China		Cold War Space Age

ENGLISH TRANSLATION OF PROVINCE NAMES

ANHUI *Peaceful Honor*

BEIJING *Northern Capital*

FUJIAN *Prosperity Found*

GANSU *Pleasant Respect*

GUANGDONG *Wide East*

GUANGXI *Wide West*

GUIZHOU *Honorable District*

HEBEI *North of the River*

HEILONGJIANG *Black Dragon River*

HENAN *South of the River*

HUBEI *North of the Lake*

HUNAN *South of the Lake*

JIANGSU *River Revival*

JIANGXI *River West*

JILIN *Magic Forest*

LIAONING *Distant Peace*

NEMENGGU *Inner Mongolia*

NINGXIA *Peaceful Summer*

QINGHAI *Turquoise Sea*

SHAANXI *West of the Pass*

SHANDONG *East of the Mountains*

SHANGHAI *On the Sea*

SHANXI *West of the Mountains*

SICHUAN *Four Rivers*

TIANJIN *Heavenly Ford*

HONG KONG (XIANGGANG) *Fragrant Harbor*

XINJIANG UYGUR *New Frontier-Uygur*

XIZANG (TIBET) *Western Treasure-house*

YUNNAN *South of the Clouds*

ZHEJIANG *Bore River*

Ürümqi ●

XINJIANG
UYGUR

XIZANG
(TIBET)

Lhasa ●

THE PEOPLE'S
REPUBLIC
OF CHINA

© 1986 A Karl/J Kemp

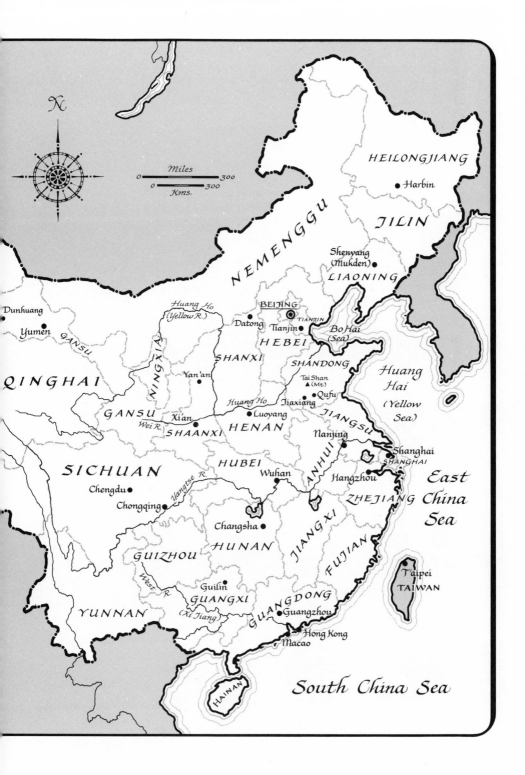

1

PREHISTORIC MYTH AND LEGEND: TO THE END OF THE XIA DYNASTY

(c 5000–c 1600 B.C.)

China, for the West, is the other side of the world—the Far East. Reverse this, and you have the Chinese view. For at least thirty centuries they have thought of their country as the center of all nations and still, today, call it the Middle Kingdom, or Zhongguo [Chung-kuo]. Hold on to this perspective if you can as you read what follows. Let the Western Hemisphere be the other side of the world for a change and think of China as the center of human activity on earth.

Imagine a time in prehistory when hunter-gatherer tribes of black-haired people, descended from the Neolithic Peking Man and his like, settled down in the Yellow River basin as they learned to fish, grow crops, and domesticate animals. This is the picture suggested by twentieth-century archeological findings in China.

We know that between 5000 and 3000 B.C., these early Yellow River communities developed a culture, named Yangshao by archeologists because the first examples of this culture were found at Yangshao village in Henan province. Toward the end of this period, while, in the West, Sumerian culture flourished in Mesopotamia, the people of the Yangshao culture fished with nets, gathered fruits and nuts, ground harvested grains with mortar and pestle, fired painted pots, and lived in round thatched homes with

1

Figure 1. The brother and sister consorts Fuxi and Nuwa, often shown with dragon tails, were the first legendary rulers. This rubbing comes from a second century A.D. stone relief carving, in the Wu family tombs in Jiaxiang, Shandong province.

their domesticated animals. They buried their dead in round pits—often with a female corpse and her best pots and other artifacts in the middle. Around her lay the corpses of men, women, and children who had died earlier and whose bodies had been temporarily buried elsewhere. This pattern suggests a matriarchal hierarchy.

In contrast, the graves of a thousand years later contain a male skeleton lying full length on its back, with one or more female skeletons on their sides facing the male figure, knees and waists bent in obeisance. This arrangement, along with newly developed wheel-thrown pottery, indicates the full fruition of a second, overlapping culture begun c 3000 B.C., with a patriarchal organization. Archeologists call it Longshan (which is also named after an archeological site).

These findings have come to light in the last hundred years and were not available to the early Chinese historiographers. Until recently their records, officially compiled sometime around the fifth century B.C., were the only source for China's ancient history. Their history began with legendary figures whose stories, passed down from earlier periods, explained the origins of the world and

2

the human race and the evolution of culture. Like early Biblical personages, Greek gods, and heroes of Western civilization, these first Chinese figures were larger-than-life prototypes who reflected the cultural priorities of those who invented them. There is no archeological proof that any of these figures existed.

Bangu [Pan-ku]

Bangu, the original human creature, is a God-Adam figure who separated heaven from earth. He and his four assistants, the dragon, the phoenix, the tortoise, and the unicorn, created all the living things on the earth. When Bangu had finished making heaven and earth, he died so that his body might become part of his creation. He was transformed into a landscape with his head becoming mountains, his flesh turning into fields and his bones into rocks. His hair became trees and grasses while his breath became the wind and clouds. The sweat of his labors poured down as rain, and, finally, the insects that clung to his body became people.

After Bangu, a legendary chronology included several generations of demigod rulers, who were followed in turn by several legendary human rulers. These rulers are not grouped consistently in the traditional histories; the version of the group known as the five legendary rulers (used in this book) combines demigods and human prototypes, each of whom represents a significant aspect of a developing society.

Fuxi [Fu-hsi] and Nuwa [Nü-wa]

Fuxi, the first of the five legendary rulers, shared his rule with his sister-consort, Nuwa. Both Fuxi and Nuwa are often shown as demigods, with human torsos and intertwined dragon tails, holding in their raised hands the symbols of their work. Fuxi taught the people to fish with nets, build homes, and care for the six traditional Chinese domesticated animals: horses, sheep, cattle, pigs, dogs, and fowl. Nuwa saved the people from the first great flood by using four turtle legs to hold up the sky, smelting rocks into five-colored stones with which she patched up the heavens, and clearing the fields and woods of flood waters by channeling the rivers.

3

Figure 2. Fuxi, first legendary ruler and inventor of writing, is repre-sented as a historical personage in this eighteenth-century portrait on silk. The Metropolitan Museum of Art, gift of Mrs. Edward S. Hark-ness, 1947

As one of the purported inventors of writing, Fuxi is a sort of patron saint of the Chinese art of calligraphy. The pictographs he is said to have devised as written symbols for speech evolved into the characters that are still used in China today. These characters mean much more to the Chinese than the letters in our alphabet mean to us. Whether printed in the newspaper or transformed into artistic expressions by a great calligrapher, each character is con-sidered an aesthetic composition, a visual image with many levels of meaning. It is as though the etymology of an English word were laid out in brilliantly drafted sketches.

4

Today we can see examples of early pictographs, similar to those attributed to Fuxi, in museum displays of oracle bones found at prehistoric sites of the third millennium B.C. Turtle shells and animal bones were heated by fire until they cracked, and an oracular significance was attributed to the shapes of the cracks; this was then recorded in pictographs scratched on the oracle bones. Later, in the second millennium B.C., pictographs on oracle bones recorded astronomic and historic events.

Fuxi is credited as the originator of another system central to Chinese civilization. One day, his legend continues, as Fuxi stood by the Yellow River, a "dragon-horse" suddenly rose from the river with a scroll on its back covered with mystical diagrams. Fuxi studied these and made of them the eight diagrams which became the basis for an orderly view of the universe and a key for divinations. This system, which was formally recorded sometime in the first millennium B.C. and which has come down to us in a book most familiarly known in translation as the *I-ching* [pinyin spelling: *Yi Jing*], has been central to philosophical and scientific thought in China. (See chapter 2, under Zhouxin; also chapter 3, under Confucius.)

Shen Nong [Shen-nung]

Shen Nong, the second legendary ruler, is called the father of Chinese agriculture and medicine. Tradition credits him with teaching the people to make plows and to recognize the best soils for planting different crops. He also studied herbs with the help of a transparent covering to his stomach that enabled him to monitor the effect of an herb on his digestive system. Shen Nong is the Chinese counterpart of the patron god of Western medicine, Aesculapius, with his healing wand in hand.

Huangdi [Huang-ti]

Huangdi ("Yellow Emperor"), the third legendary ruler, fought his way to ascendancy over a number of the tribes in the central Yellow River valley to establish the first version of a Chinese state. He was said to have lived in a palace with a court that included astronomer-historians who built an observatory, established a calendar, and kept records of significant celestial and terrestrial events. Beyond the palace walls, Huangdi supposedly taught his subjects to work the land with ox-drawn carts and plows; we see here the rise of two distinct classes, the bureaucrats, who assisted the ruler inside the palace, and the peasants, who farmed the land. They would be the mainstays of China's social structure until the middle of the twentieth century. (Many insist they still are, despite the reforms of the People's Republic.)

Huangdi's wife, Leizu [Lei-tsu], was the first empress. Legend credits her with one of China's most important industries: silk culture. One spring day, the story goes, she was walking in the palace garden with her handmaidens when she noticed silkworm cocoons on the leaves of mulberry trees. She was entranced by the fine filament that went around and around the cocoons and had her handmaidens gather some cocoons and put them in water to see if the filaments could be softened and removed. The empress took a comb from her hair to stir the cocoons. When she lifted the comb, the ends of the fine filaments had caught on to the comb's teeth. She turned the comb as she drew it back from the floating cocoons, thereby twisting the filaments into the first spun silk thread. Before long the empress and her handmaidens had spun enough threads to weave a cloth and make an imperial robe. After this, silkworms and mulberry trees were cultivated for silk production, and subsequent empresses honored Leizu's invention by gathering cocoons in an annual spring festival.

When silk culture actually began in China is unknown, but we do know that it was well established by about the fifteenth century B.C. The Chinese exported silk, as a finished product, over the first Silk Road to Rome during the first century B.C., but it was not until the sixth century A.D. that silk was manufactured outside of China. It was then that two Nestorian priests, members of a Christian sect that developed in Constantinople in the sixth century and the first to send missionaries to China, returned home with silkworms hidden inside bamboo canes. From Constantinople, silk culture and production spread throughout Europe and flourished particularly in Italy.

With Huangdi the Chinese state was invented. Next came the question of how it should be governed. The answer is given in the examples of the last two of the five legendary rulers, Yao and Shun, as well as that of their successor, Yu, who was the first ruler to establish a dynasty. Together these three were considered *the* models of virtuous leadership for all future rulers to emulate.

If we look for a moment at the written character that stands for the Chinese word meaning "law," we can grasp the key to this trio's leadership. The character is made of two parts: on the left side is the symbol for "water" and on the right side the symbol for "go." The idea of law in China is directly associated with flood prevention and irrigation, with making the "water go" in manageable and predictable channels.

Figure 3

Nuwa, Fuxi's dragon-tailed sister-consort, was the first flood controller. From now on this role would be given to the rulers of the state as their first duty in maintaining a well-ordered society. Yao, Shun, and Yu share the credit for their attempts to control floods, thereby bringing prosperity to their subjects.

Yao

Yao, the fourth legendary ruler, was said to have been born fourteen months after his mother observed a red dragon. However, as ruler he did not use this illustrious birth to aggrandize himself but instead refused the titles of emperor and king and devoted himself to the welfare of his people. He placed a drum and a tablet outside the palace gates so that anyone with a grievance could bang the drum and tell Yao of his troubles or write his advice on the tablet.

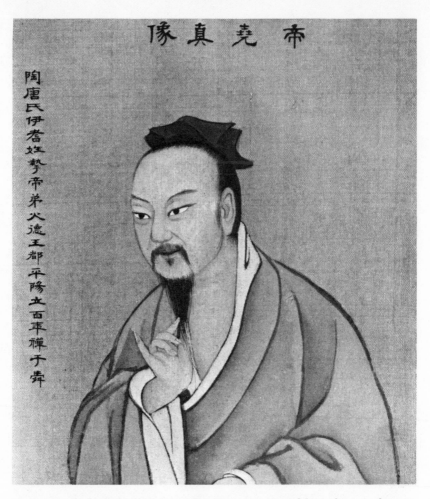

Figure 4. The fourth legendary ruler, Yao, encouraged his subjects to bang the drum outside his palace when they had cause to complain. The Metropolitan Museum of Art, gift of Mrs. Edward S. Harkness, 1947

Shun

The legends state that during Yao's rule a period of terrible floods occurred, and Yao asked his people if there was anyone among them who could help to stay the waters. Shun's name was suggested. Shun, at that time, was known as a model of filial devotion and industriousness. When his stepmother and half brother and even his father tried to throw him down a well, Shun forgave them all and went on working at their side. His virtuous reputation won

8

the respect of many, who moved to live near him, and soon his village grew into a town and then into a city.

Shun, responding to Yao's call for help with the flooding waters, worked with such diligence that Yao gave him his daughter in marriage and named him his heir.

Shun, last of the five legendary rulers, was not able to complete the task of bringing the floods under control, so he sought someone to carry on his work. He chose Yu, who studied the contours of the land and the patterns of water flow and devised a new system of rerouting the river in some places, of dredging it in others, and of building canals. Shun made Yu his heir.

The stories of Yao, Shun, and Yu indicate that China's chronic problems with water control have required constant attention over the last three thousand years. The Yellow River has, in fact, been rerouted many times in attempts to stop its enormous floodings; most recently this was done in the 1940s. The network of canals in China, the best known of which is the Grand Canal built in the sixth and seventh centuries, is still vital to both irrigation and transportation.

Figure 5. The Yellow River delta as seen in a recent photograph. Yue Guofang, New China Pictures Co.

Figure 6. This is one of over a thousand ditches dug in the farmlands of Henan province in recent years for irrigation and drainage of Yellow River waters. Fan Mingtao, New China Pictures Co.

Figure 7. The "dragon-backbone machine," as the Chinese call this foot-powered pallet and chain pump, has been a common water mover since at least the second century A.D.

The Xia [Hsia] Dynasty
c 2100–c 1600 B.C.

Yu

Yu, who succeeded Shun, is a pivotal figure in the ancient Chinese legends. He is grouped with Yao and Shun as one of three model rulers, but because he chose his own son as his heir, he was also the first ruler to start a dynasty. (A dynasty is the continual rule by members of one family.)

This first Chinese dynasty, called Xia, though legendary, is nonetheless dated c 2100 to c 1600 B.C., and is supposed to have had seventeen kings. Recent archeological excavations eighteen miles east of present-day Luoyang [Lo-yang] ("North of the River Luo") (see map 3) suggest that Yangcheng, one of the supposed capitals of this dynasty, may have been an actual city. If this is substantiated, then the Xia rulers may move from legend into history.

Yu, as first king of the Xia dynasty, earned his reputation as a virtuous ruler by devoting all his time to the welfare of his people. His kingdom, we are told, was divided into feudal states, all of which were content under his benevolent rule. His heirs, unfortunately, did not share his high-minded zeal and became increasingly corrupt and degenerate until, with the seventeenth and last of these, we meet the first Chinese tyrant, the legendary Jie.

Jie [Chie]

Jie cared not in the least about the good of his people but rather spent his time in orgies and amusements conducted at their expense. Together with a slave girl, who became his favorite consort, he devised ever new excesses, such as the lake of wine in which subjects were forced to plunge thousands at a time to the beat of a drum while the king and his consort laughed at their forced and tortured intoxication.

While Jie indulged in such dissipations, his unhappy subjects turned to the Lord of Shang, the just ruler of one of the feudal

11

states, and asked him to rid them of the terrible tyrant. The legends report that the planets wandered off their courses and mountains fell into rivers until the Lord of Shang was persuaded that it was correct for him to challenge the king. A great battle was fought, Jie was banished, to die soon after, and the Lord of Shang took the throne and declared a new dynasty.

The pattern established in the legendary Xia dynasty introduces a sequence that recurred again and again in Chinese history. After an initial period of strong leadership and good works, a dynasty began to falter as the rulers grew increasingly corrupt and lost what became known as the Mandate of Heaven, that is, they ceased to put their people's welfare before their own. This abuse of leadership became the justification for replacing the old dynasty with a new one, through invasion from the outside or rebellion from within or a combination of both. A new leader emerged and invoked the Mandate of Heaven to legitimize his family's rule. The succession from ruler to ruler within a dynasty did not necessarily follow from father to oldest son. Frequently a younger son, grandson, or nephew was designated heir to the throne. This contrasts with the rule of primogeniture in European princely houses.

2

HISTORY BEGINS: THE SHANG AND WESTERN ZHOU DYNASTIES

c 1600–771 B.C.

The Shang Dynasty
c 1600–c 1100

Tang [T'ang]

The Lord of Shang, who claimed the Mandate of Heaven from the last Xia ruler, is known as Tang, and he gave his new dynasty the name of his vassal state, Shang. Its history is based on pictographic inscriptions on oracle bones (see chapter 2, Fuxi), bamboo slips, bronze artifacts, and even an occasional silk remnant.

A calendar developed during the Shang period became the basis for the traditional Chinese calendar still used today. A solar year of 365 days is combined with a year of twelve lunar months, or 360 days, and every few years an extra month is added to make these two types of year match. According to the Shang inscriptions, the Shang dynasty lasted about five hundred years, with thirty-one kings, and had several successive capitals, the best known and last of which was at Anyang (see map 2).

If we make an approximate match of the dates for the Shang dynastic records with the dates of the Gregorian calendar used in the West (and now also by the Chinese side by side with their

13

*Shang (c 1600–c 1100 B.C.) and Western Zhou
(c 1100–771 B.C.) Dynasties*

own), we find that during the five centuries of Shang rule, the great
Minoan palaces on Crete were mysteriously destroyed, Tutankh-
amen lived (and died) in golden splendor in Egypt, Stonehenge
was completed in the British Isles, the Greeks won the Trojan
War, and Moses led his people across the desert to the Promised
Land.

Tang, first king of this dynasty, was known as a superb ruler;
he followed the august examples of Yao, Shun, and Yu and certainly kept his Mandate from Heaven. When a seven-year drought
brought famine to the land, Tang took this as a sign that heaven
was displeased with his rule. The story goes that he dressed himself
in white mourning robes (white is the traditional color for mourning

14

Figure 8. Tang, the Lord of Shang, founded China's first historically authenticated dynasty. The Metropolitan Museum of Art, gift of Mrs. Edward S. Harkness, 1947

in China) and went out to the foot of a great mountain, where he knelt with his forehead to the ground and cried out all his sins and those of his people. When he was done, there was a clap of thunder, and rain poured down from heaven, bringing the crops back to life.

Tang sought the help of a learned man named Yi Yin [I Yin], known for his expertise in cultivation, sending him three invitations before Yi agreed to become prime minister. Yi helped prevent further famine by teaching the peasants to cultivate seeds in shallow pits irrigated by hand. He was also known as a great chef.

15

His enemies claimed that his influence on Tang derived from his ability to cook!

We can imagine Yi Yin overseeing not only the royal table but also the preparations for ceremonial occasions when, today, we admire the magnificent bronze vessels of the Shang period in museum collections. Extraordinary skill went into making these goblets, pitchers, and cauldrons. The largest of the latter, some weighing close to a ton, required not only sophisticated metallurgy but also the coordinated efforts of several hundred skilled workers.

The shapes and relief designs of these vessels evolved from quite realistic to very stylized animal forms. One easily recognized motif in the more stylized patterns is that of two raised knobs symbolizing the eyes of the taotie, or glutton, mask (for more on this see appendix II). Inscriptions on many of the vessels indicate that the king used them during seasonal ceremonies when he offered grain and sacrificed animals to heaven and earth with prayers for a bountiful harvest.

Shang archeological sites reveal that architecture in China has

Figure 9. This three-legged Shang bronze ceremonial vessel (twelfth century B.C.) is called a ting and shows a fine example of the taotie (glutton mask) on its surface. Courtesy of the Freer Gallery of Art, Smithsonian Institution, Washington, D.C.

been extraordinarily consistent over the past three thousand years. Rectangular wooden structures were built on a foundation of pounded earth. The orientation of throne platforms, doors, and gates was always to the south. Today's visitor to the Forbidden City in Beijing [Pei-ching or, conventionally in the West, Peking] will see the same overall rectangular plan with the main gate and all the important ceremonial buildings facing south. Chinese rulers looked to the south while their subjects turned northward to face them. A similar tradition, which may come down from Shang times, is for a host to sit facing south with the most important guest on his left, to the east.

The rich and highly organized Bronze Age culture of the Shang did not ensure the dynasty's survival. Tang's virtuous example was not followed by successive kings, with the predictable outcome of corruption and lost power. Under the tyrant Zhouxin, the dynasty fell altogether.

Zhouxin [Chou-hsin]

Zhouxin (in some texts he is referred to as Dixin), last king of Shang, was perversely evil, but he considered himself a genius. Physically he had the strength of a wild beast and bested them in combat. He listened to no one. Once, when his uncle, a learned man devoted to the public good, made a rational proposal, Zhouxin became so enraged that he ordered his guards to rip out the uncle's heart. He afterward claimed that he had heard that the heart of a wise man had seven openings, and his uncle's heart would prove the truth or falsity of this.

In his palace Zhouxin kept dogs and horses, and the decor was strange: Wine was used to fill up artificial ponds and meat was hung to resemble a forest. His love of women was prodigious, but he had a favorite: a beautiful slave girl who rose to power through her encouragement of the king's pursuits and for whom he built an enormous tower. Their preferred entertainment was watching an accused person prove his innocence or guilt by trying to cross a well-greased metal column laid over a pit of burning coals. If he fell in, he was guilty; if he reached the other side, innocent.

When the ruler of a vassal state voiced an objection to the

17

tyrant's cruelties, he was seized and put in prison. This man, known as the Duke of Zhou (not to be confused with Zhouxin, the tyrant), is a revered figure in Chinese history. He supposedly spent his time in prison studying the eight mystical diagrams of the legendary Fuxi, and elaborating additional diagrams and meanings for use in divination and the interpretation of natural phenomena (see chapter 1, Fuxi; also chapter 3, Confucius). After seven years he was finally set free when his son paid a huge ransom, and he returned to rule his vassal state. When he died, this same son sought the help of other vassal rulers and, in a great and celebrated battle, challenged and defeated the infamous Zhouxin. This latter fled to his palace, dressed himself in all his jewels, set the palace on fire, and jumped into the flames from his mistress's tower. She escaped the flames but was captured and beheaded.

The Western Zhou [Chou] Dynasty

c 1100–771 B.C.

Zhou Wuwang [Chou Wu-wang]

The son of the Duke of Zhou, who defeated the last ruler of the Shang dynasty, took the title Wuwang ("Martial King"), founded the Zhou dynasty, named after his father's dukedom, and moved the capital westward to Hao, slightly south of present-day Xi'an. (The capitals of the Chinese dynasties moved back and forth frequently after this, from the area around Luoyang in the east to the area around Xi'an in the west, depending on the power base of the dynasty. Beijing, the present capital, was not used as China's capital until the thirteenth century.) Twelve Zhou kings ruled from Hao over a period of more than three hundred years.

Dan, Duke of Zhou

Zhou Wuwang had a brother who is revered by the Chinese as one of the three great sages. (The other two were Yu, controller of the flooding waters and founder of the Xia dynasty, and Confucius, the sixth-century philosopher.) This brother inherited his father's

周武王真像

姬姓名發嗣位十三年都鎬在位七年

Figure 10. Zhou Wuwang defeated the last Shang ruler and claimed the Mandate of Heaven for a new dynasty. The Metropolitan Museum of Art, gift of Mrs. Edward S. Harkness, 1947

title and is known as Dan, Duke of Zhou. He is remembered as a great scholar-inventor who used his learning in the service of his king and the effective rule of the kingdom. He continued the study of the mystical diagrams which his father had begun in prison. He helped his brother, the king, in the roles of prime minister and general, and when his brother died, he did not take the throne, as many suspected he would, but served a nephew who became king. An extraordinary inventor, he was credited with making the first known compass. This was an ingenious mechanical (rather than magnetic) device, fixed to the front of a chariot, which always managed to hold a south-pointing position. The first account of its use tells of some envoys to the capital being sent home to their lands in what is now Vietnam, guided by this magical pointer.

The Zhou inherited from the Shang the techniques of bronze casting, silk culture, and animal breeding. On one of their bronze vessels is an inscription that records the trading of five slaves for a horse and a hank of silk. This inscription, which can be seen today in the Museum of History in Beijing, is one documentation of slavery during this time. Probably the custom began during the Shang dynasty when prisoners of war were made slaves, but the records are not clear.

By the mid-eighth century B.C., when, in the West, Homer is said to have lived and Rome was founded on the Tiber, the Zhou dynasty, like the Shang before it, had weakened under corrupt rulers and almost ended with the third tyrant of Chinese history— and yet another demanding consort.

You [Yu]

The twelfth Zhou ruler, You fell in love with a beautiful concubine whom he made his queen; he sought endlessly to amuse her. The first recorded eclipse of the sun occurred during You's reign, in 775 B.C. His subjects took the eclipse as a sign that heaven was displeased with their ruler, but he ignored this portent and devoted himself to spoiling his queen. She loved the sound of tearing silk, so he ordered his slaves to rip up yards and yards of imperial brocade. This activity merely depleted the palace wardrobes while the queen grew bored and sullen. You, desperate to devise further amusements, ordered the beacons lit and the drums to sound, the traditional signals of an approaching enemy. The alarmed militia arrived in haste to protect the kingdom only to find the queen laughing in their assembled faces. Later, in 771 B.C., when barbarian tribes from the west attacked the capital of Hao, the beacons were lit and the drums sounded in earnest; the warriors thought it another trick and did not come. King You was taken prisoner, and the queen strangled herself. The rule of the Western Zhou ended when the rest of the Zhou court fled eastward and established a new capital at Luoyang.

From this now thrice-occurring story of dynastic downfall, first in the legendary Xia and then again in the Shang and Western Zhou, comes the tradition of the Three Great Beauties, the three women who aided and abetted the last tyrannical rulers of these dynasties. (Some add a fourth beauty to the list, a lady we will meet in the Tang dynasty.) An ancient ode records their legacy:

> *A wise man builds up the city wall,*
> *A wise woman overthrows it. . . .*
> *A woman with a long tongue*
> *Is a stepping-stone to disorder.*
> *Disorder does not come from heaven;*
> *It is produced by a woman.*[1]

It is necessary to mention another chronic cause of disruption in China, one which in the long run caused much more grief than wayward queens and which was evident in the downfall of the Western Zhou. This was the presence along the northern and western borders of nomadic tribes who lived by herding livestock and periodically raided the agricultural settlements and rich cities of the Chinese. The Chinese devised two basic strategies for protecting themselves. They fought against the invaders in armed combat from defensive fortifications; they also kept them at bay by offering them gifts and tributary status.

It is essential to remember that the Chinese considered themselves the center of the civilized world and all those beyond their borders barbarians. The integrity of their Middle Kingdom would be best preserved by keeping all foreigners out. This attitude has characterized China's foreign diplomacy throughout her history; it has also helped the Chinese state to prevail after periods of internal disunity, such as that which followed the disruption of Western Zhou rule, or after periods of foreign rule.

1. James Legge, *Chinese Classics* (Oxford: Clarendon Press, 1872), 4: 561.

3

THE EASTERN ZHOU DYNASTY AND THE FIRST PERIOD OF DISUNITY

770–221 B.C.

T he Zhou rule, greatly weakened by the invasion of nomadic "barbarian" tribes who took over the capital of Hao and surrounding western lands, continued more in name than in fact from a new, eastern capital, Luoyang, as the kingdom broke up into vassal states with nominal allegiance to the Zhou king. Between 770 and 221 B.C. these vassal states grew increasingly independent, while the territory actually governed by the Zhou shrank to a little circle around Luoyang.

The years from 770 to 476 B.C. are known as the Spring and Autumn period. This poetic name is taken from the *Spring and Autumn Annals*, a history of this period written in the fifth century B.C. and based on the records kept each spring and autumn of celestial, ceremonial, political, and other significant events. The authorship of this history is traditionally attributed to Confucius.

The Warring States period follows, from 475 to 221 B.C., so called because the separate states were endlessly fighting against one another and the Zhou rule. A look at the map of China in this period illustrates this clearly. In the middle is a tiny area around the capital, Luoyang, which was the real property of the Zhou rulers. Surrounding this, the much larger shapes of the Warring States all but squeeze out this center. These states pretended

Warring States (475–221 B.C.)

allegiance to the Zhou kings but in fact were rival principalities.
Their rulers, who at first called themselves princes or dukes, began
to take the title king, thereby challenging the authority of the Zhou
kings. At times several states might band together in combat against
nomadic tribes to the north or west, but mostly they waged war
among themselves.

These five centuries of political instability, during which debate
among philosophers trying to answer the age-old questions about
man's role and function in the universe produced the Hundred
Schools of Thought, are considered China's golden age of philosophy. During this period, three major doctrines evolved: Confucianism, Daoism, and Legalism. Confucianism, after the first century
B.C., became China's authoritative guide to political and social
behavior; Daoism became her only native religion; and Legalism,

which had the most immediate and profound effect on the history of the third century B.C., continued thereafter to influence her legal codes.

Confucius (551–479 B.C.), his disciple Mencius (active 372–289 B.C.), and Laozi, father of Daoism (sixth century B.C.), are the great, world-renowned trio of Chinese philosophy. The lesser known Shang Yang (fourth century B.C.) is considered the father of Legalism. Their lives were roughly contemporaneous to those of Gautama, the Buddha, in India (c 560 B.C.), Zoroaster in Iran (c 600 B.C.), and Socrates (469–399 B.C.), Plato (427–347 B.C.), and Aristotle (384–322 B.C.) in Greece.

The Great Philosophers

Confucius [pinyin: Kongzi; Wade-Giles: K'ung Fu-tzu]

Confucius (whose name in Chinese means Master Kung) was born in 551 B.C. in the small state of Lu, one of the vassal states of the Spring and Autumn period. (Today one can visit the town of his birth and death, Qufu [Chü-fu], in Shandong province, filled with the commemorating shrines of later ages.) He was a precocious student of historical and ceremonial lore who rose to an unusually high government position for someone not of royal birth and then resigned from his post as a protest against the misrule of his prince. Confucius left the state of Lu and, accompanied by his disciples, traveled to other states, seeking service under a prince he deemed more worthy. After several years of wandering, he concluded that his quest was futile, so he returned to his native Lu and spent the years until his death, in 479 B.C., collecting and editing the most important writings of earlier periods of Chinese history into five volumes known as the Five Classics.

We do not know how much of these Five Classics was actually compiled or authored by Confucius. Certainly his teachings dominate their contents, for Confucius was first and foremost a teacher. In fact, he was China's first known professional educator. He turned to legend, ritual song, and history to find models of proper human conduct—conduct where mutual respect guided the rela-

先師孔子行教像

德侔天地
道冠古今

刪述六經
垂憲萬世

Figure 11. Confucius is the latinized name for China's foremost philosopher. His teachings became state orthodoxy in the second century B.C. and dominated Chinese society for the next two thousand years. This traditional representation is from a stone rubbing. Courtesy of the Museum of Fine Arts, Boston

tions between ruler and subject, man and man, husband and wife, and parent and child. Confucius believed profoundly that men of all social levels could learn, through knowledge of past examples and practice of ritual, to become humane and virtuous participants in a harmonious social hierarchy. Man was an uncarved block who needed to be shaped by education into the moral being who would place concern for others ahead of all thought of personal gain. Thus, the moral monarch would gain the allegiance of his subjects through his benevolent rule and the same pattern would apply to the other above-mentioned relationships. In the centuries immediately following his death, Confucius's ideas were distorted by the Legalists, who used them to justify strict laws giving absolute authority to rulers, husbands, and fathers. His premise of social order established through mutual respect was turned into order maintained by threat of punishment.

25

The Five Classics

1. *Shu Jing [Shu-ching] ("Book of History")*: This book collects historical reports of the early dynasties, such as the stories of Yao, Shun, and Yu, and presents them as moral lessons in political behavior.

2. *Shi Jing [Shih-ching] ("Book of Odes,"* or *"Book of Songs")*: Some of these odes date back to the Zhou, and perhaps even the Shang, dynasty. Many are intended for use during ceremonial sacrifices and other ritual functions, while others celebrate or comment on quotidian events.

3. *Li Ji [Li-chi] ("Record of Ritual")*: This is the guide to proper social behavior that all men and women ought to follow.

4. *Yi Jing [I-ching] ("Book of Changes")* (We will use the Wade-Giles spelling still used as the title for most translations): Here is the book of diagrams and their interpretations said to originate in the scroll on the back of the "dragon-horse" which appeared before the legendary Fuxi. They are more reliably traced back to the twelfth century B.C., when, it is said, the Duke of Zhou spent his seven-year imprisonment developing an elaborate system of sixty-four diagrams and their meanings. (See chapter 1, Fuxi; chapter 2, Zhouxin.)

The diagrams are composed of two basic elements: a straight line and a broken line. The first symbolizes a force called yang, indicating the positive, the sun, south, light, heaven, male; the second, the broken line, symbolizes yin, indicating the negative, the moon, north, darkness, the earth, female. Neither force can exist without the other; we cannot know light without dark; duality is present in all we know or observe. In the Judeo-Christian tradition, duality is seen as a fight between Good and Evil in which Good should prevail. With yin and yang, the notion of duality is quite different; these forces must balance for the world to be in harmony.

In the diagrams, the yin and the yang lines are combined first into eight different sets of three parallel lines, which are called trigrams, and then into sixty-four sets of six parallel lines, called hexagrams. The eight trigrams symbolize, among other things, the elements and cardinal directions, while the sixty-four hexagrams

1	2	3	4	5	6	7	8
male	lake	fire	thunder	wind	rain	mountain	female
heaven	water	sun			moon		earth

Figure 12. Top: *The eight trigrams used in the* I-ching *represent basic elements of nature.* Right: *They also can be interpreted as symbols of direction. The divisions of the inner circle represent the yin (black, feminine) and the yang (white, masculine) forces in the universe.*

were used to interpret natural phenomena or prescribe the conduct of human affairs on all levels.

(Another representation of the dual forces of yin and yang is the circle evenly divided by an *S*.)

5. *Chun Qiu [Ch'un-ch'iu] ("Spring and Autumn Annals")*: This history of the state of Lu from 722–476 B.C. is said to have been compiled and edited by Confucius. Three commentaries, written by three different authors, were added soon after as interpretations of his selections.

There was said to be a sixth classic, the *Book of Music*, which did not survive the great burning of books at the end of the third century B.C.

After Confucius's death, his own writings and teachings were collected and, later, with the teachings of Mencius, made into what are known as the Four Books. These were:

1. *Lun Yu [Lun-yü] ("Analects")*: Here, collected by his disciples, are the sayings and conversations of Confucius, which embody the ideals of the virtuous man (as shown in the following examples):

The Master said, "The sage and the man of perfect virtue; how dare I rank myself with them? It may simply be said

27

of me, that I strive to become such without satiety, and teach others without weariness. . . ."[1]

To be able to practice five things everywhere under heaven constitutes perfect virtue. . . . [These are] gravity, generosity of soul, sincerity, earnestness and kindness. If you are grave, you will not be treated with disrespect. If you are generous, you will win all. If you are sincere, people will repose trust in you. If you are earnest, you will accomplish much. If you are kind, this will enable you to employ the service of others.[2]

2. *Da Xue [Ta-hsüeh]* (*"Great Learning"*): This work, whose commentaries may have been written by a disciple of Confucius's, sets forth a concept of government based on the virtue of rulers.

What is meant by "In order rightly to govern the state, it is necessary first to regulate the family" is this:—It is not possible for one to teach others, while he cannot teach his own family. Therefore, the ruler, without going beyond his family, completes the lessons for the state. There is filial piety:—therewith the sovereign should be served. There is fraternal submission:—therewith elders and superiors should be served. There is kindness:—therewith the multitude should be treated.[3]

3. *Zhong Yong [Chung-yung]* (*"Doctrine of the Mean"*): A Confucian ideal that embraces every relationship and activity of one's life, the doctrine of the mean prescribes regulation and moderation in all things. Only thus can one achieve a state of mental balance and harmony. The book, ascribed to Confucius's grandson, but also containing material thought to have been added in the third century B.C., opens with these lines:

1. James Legge, trans., *The Four Books* (New York: Paragon Book Reprint Corp., 1966), 93.
2. Ibid., 257 ff.
3. Ibid., 329.

What Heaven has conferred is called THE NATURE; an accordance with this nature is called THE PATH of duty; the regulation of this path is called INSTRUCTION.[4]

Further on, the legendary ruler Shun is presented as an example:

The Master said, "There was Shun:—He indeed was greatly wise! Shun loved to question others, and to study their words, though they might be shallow. He concealed what was bad in them, and displayed what was good. He took hold of their two extremes, determined the Mean, and employed it in his government of the people. It was by this that he was Shun!"[5]

4. *Mengzi [Meng-tzu] (Mencius)*: The conversations about responsible government between Mencius and the princes of the Warring States were taken down and collected by Mencius's disciples (see below, Mencius).

Since the Five Classics and the Four Books became the core of Chinese education, we will interrupt our chronology to consider a brief outline of this development. The first official sanction of Confucianism as government creed came in the second century B.C., when the Han dynasty emperor Wudi sought out Confucian scholars to serve in his government. He instituted competitive examinations as a means of recruiting men of ability and encouraged the study of the classics as preparation for these tests. Much later, in the seventh century, under the Tang dynasty emperor Taizong, state schools were established in which the study of the Confucian classics was the central curriculum and recruitment through examination became more rigidly systematized. From then on, with the exception of the Mongol era, Chinese politics and education were completely dominated by Confucian doctrine and the examination system.

In these later centuries, students (almost without exception

4. Ibid., 349.
5. Ibid., 356.

these were boys) began at age five to memorize the Four Books and the Five Classics; if they succeeded, they went on, as adolescents, to the detailed study of a vast body of commentary on these and to take the first of many levels of examinations. Moving up examination by examination, each one of which could be taken any number of times, an ultimately tiny percentage of these students succeeded, in their mid-thirties, in passing the last of them and receiving the most coveted administrative posts. Underlying this fiercely competitive arrangement was the conviction that a complete knowledge of Confucian doctrine, which emphasized moral behavior, filial piety, and devotion to imperial ritual, was the only appropriate training for scholar-officials.

One result of this system of education was a certain social mobility. Although a self-perpetuating class of scholar-official families developed, it was also the case that men of humbler origins could occasionally, through diligent study, rise to high rank. It must be said, however, that for every one of those who succeeded, there were thousands who spent their lives repeatedly failing the examinations.

Confucian scholar-officials (called mandarins by Westerners; the word comes from the Portuguese version of a Malay word, *mantri*, meaning "minister of state"), whose rank was indicated by an elaborate system of color-coded robes, served at every level of government and were shapers of civic, economic, and military policy. Many were also great poets, painters, and calligraphers, honored as much for their reputation in the arts as for their role in government.

Although, by the first century B.C., Confucius was accorded the status of a supernatural being and temples were built in his honor, it is misleading to compare Confucianism to Christianity. Confucianism is essentially an ethical code for social behavior rather than a religious faith. The first concern of a Confucian is his fellow man, not a deity, and Confucius is not considered the son of God. Worship in a Confucian temple is based on an ancient tradition of ritualistic ancestor worship, a tradition that the Master encouraged and enhanced; his teachings are a great sage's words of wisdom rather than divine revelation. Furthermore, being a

Confucianist did not stop anyone from also being a Daoist, a Buddhist, or even a Christian.

Laozi [Lao-tse]

Laozi ("Old Teacher"), the founder of Daoism, was perhaps a real person who lived during the sixth century B.C.; the accounts of his life are unreliable and full of legend. When his mother gave birth, it is said, her son had been eighty years in her womb and emerged with white hair and eyebrows. The most reliable source for his life is the great historian of the first century B.C., Sima Qian (see chapter 5), who wrote that Laozi was the librarian to a prince of the Spring and Autumn period. According to Sima Qian, he was dismayed by the decadence of court life and left his position to travel west, away from the society he so disliked. As he went through the border pass of his prince's state, he was recognized by the guard, a man of learning, who asked him to write down his teachings before he disappeared into self-imposed exile. (Another account says the guard set a dish of tea before the old man and that this was the origin of social tea drinking.) Laozi wrote the famous text attributed to him, *Daode Jing [Tao-te Ching]* (*"The Dao and Its Power"*), and went on his way. There is no account of his death.

The book is short and full of poetic and paradoxical statements about the dao [tao] (usually translated as "the way"), which man must follow in order to live in harmony with nature. The dao is also the "mother of all things," a primal cause or source of energy. Laozi encouraged men to return to a simple life, free of ambition, for only when men live spontaneously, without striving, do they fulfill their natural role:

Not to value and employ men of superior ability is the way to keep the people from rivalry among themselves. . . . The sage, in the exercise of his government, empties [the people's] minds, fills their bellies, weakens their wills, and strengthens their bones. He constantly [tries to] keep them without knowledge and without desire, and where there are those who have knowledge, to keep them from presuming to act [on it]. When there is this abstinence from action, good order is universal.[6]

What makes a great state is its being [like] a low-lying, down-flowing [stream]:—it becomes the centre to which tend [all the small states] under heaven.[7]

[It is the way of the tao] to act without [thinking of] acting; to conduct affairs without [feeling the] trouble of them; to taste without discerning any flavour; to consider what is small as great, and a few as many; and to recompense injury with kindness.[8]

There is a famous story about Confucius seeking out the aging Laozi in which Confucius complains that he has been seeking the dao for twenty years without success. Laozi is said to have answered, "If tao could be offered to men, there is no one who would not willingly offer it to his prince . . . present it to his parents . . . announce it to his brothers . . . transmit it to his children. Why then can you not obtain it? This is the reason. You are incapable of giving it an asylum in your heart."[9]

An interpretation of this vignette must take into account that the term *dao* was used by both Daoists and Confucians but with quite distinct meanings. Most simply stated, the dao of Laozi is the path we must follow to be in harmony with the natural order, while that of Confucius is the path we must follow to become a virtuous member of the social order.

Daoism, taken up and expanded by philosophers of the fourth century B.C., became increasingly preoccupied with cosmology, alchemy, and magic. Daoist monks offered emperor after emperor their alchemical concoctions as "elixirs of immortality." When Buddhism, which came to China from India in the first century

6. James Legge, trans., *The Texts of Taoism* (New York: Dover Publications, 1962), 1: 49.
7. Ibid., 104.
8. Ibid., 106.
9. James Legge's translation, as quoted in S. Wells Williams, *The Middle Kingdom* (New York: Charles Scribner's Sons, 1883), 212–213.

Figure 13. The founders of China's three religions, from left to right, the Buddha, Confucius, and Laozi, were contemporaries in the sixth century B.C. The reunion shown here is ecumenical fancy: Though Confucius and Laozi may conceivably have met, Buddhism was not introduced into China from India until six hundred years later. This painting on silk was done by an unknown artist of the Ming (1368–1644) dynasty. The Nelson-Atkins Museum of Art, Kansas City, Missouri, given in memory of John B. Trevor (1878–1956) by his son, Bronson Trevor

A.D., became widespread, Daoists adopted the Buddhist concept of heaven and acquired a pantheon of immortals and a Daoist trinity, which included Laozi. Despite this, Daoism is considered China's only indigenous religion.

Mencius [pinyin: *Mengzi*; Wade-Giles: *Meng-tzu*]

Mencius, the last of the three great philosophers, came from the state of Zhou, in what is now Shandong province, and was active from 372 to 289 B.C., during the Warring States period. The story of his upbringing is well known to every Chinese and serves as an example for the responsible parent. He lived with his widowed mother near a butcher shop and came home one day trying to imitate the butcher cutting up meat. His mother, alarmed that her son would become a callous child, moved to a house near a cemetery. Again the boy began to imitate what he saw next door, this time the weeping and wailing of mourners. The anxious mother moved once more, to a home opposite a school. Here the young

Mencius embarked on the study of the Confucian teachings and other classics, and finally his mother was satisfied.

Mencius's studies continued until he was forty, and then he, like Confucius before him, tried to teach the precepts of good government to the princes of his time. He taught that man was essentially good and that the ruler of men is really their servant, providing for their material and moral welfare.

> Benevolence is man's mind, and righteousness is man's path. How lamentable is it to neglect the path and not pursue it, to lose this mind and not know to seek it again!
> When men's fowls and dogs are lost, they know to seek for them again, but they lose their mind, and do not know to seek for it. The great end of learning is nothing else but to seek for the lost mind. [10]

Mencius believed that along with the lost mind, the lost art of good government could be retrieved if rulers would recapture their lost good natures. Confucius never stated what man's original nature was, but he believed man could be educated to become moral and virtuous; his disciple professed man to be innately good and that his duty was to return to this original state.

Finally we come to the Legalists, who, more than any of the other philosophers discussed above, influenced the immediate course of their own history. In reaction to the idealistic optimism of Confucius and Mencius, they stated that social order could only be maintained through strictly enforced laws. A ruler need not be a moral leader; rather, he should have complete power to enforce the law through harsh punishment.

Shang Yang

Shang Yang (fourth century B.C.) was the first well-known Legalist and is remembered as the one who prepared the way for unifying the Warring States into the first great Chinese empire. Where his contemporary Mencius preached benevolent leadership, Shang

10. James Legge, trans., *The Four Books* (New York: Paragon Book Reprint Corp., 1966), 879.

Yang advocated the absolute authority of the ruler over a centralized state.

Shang Yang began his career as a brilliant young man in the
government of the state of Wei (and is therefore sometimes referred
to as Wei Yang). The king of Wei was advised by his dying prime
minister, Shang Yang's mentor, either to promote the young scholar
or to execute him so he would not seek to serve a rival king, but
when the prime minister died, the king of Wei decided that Shang
Yang was too young for promotion. Shang Yang did not wait around
to be killed. He fled westward, in 361 B.C., to the rival state of
Qin [Ch'in] (built up by the nomadic tribes that had conquered
the old Western Zhou capital of Hao). In the service of the ruler
of Qin, Shang Yang created a strong centralized state supported
by a well-trained army and strictly kept laws.

This authoritarian regime was at first widely resisted by all,
from the peasants to the ruler's son, the crown prince. Shang Yang
did not dare to make an example of the crown prince by punishing
him directly, but he made an example of the prince's two tutors,
accusing them of not properly instructing their pupil, and branded
them both on the face. This startling punishment stifled all resistance to the new laws. The state of Qin stabilized and, with its
ruthlessly disciplined army of infantry and cavalry, became a
powerful threat to its neighbors.

Shang Yang led the Qin army against his native state of Wei,
which he conquered and brought under Qin domination. He would
no doubt have continued such conquests, but his career came
suddenly to an ironic end. In 338 B.C., the crown prince inherited
the Qin throne and his disfigured tutors persuaded him to order
their torturer's arrest. Shang Yang tried to escape across the Qin
border but had to stop at an inn on the way. One of the laws he
had instituted required any man traveling through the state to carry
a passport to be shown to innkeepers with whom they might lodge.
When Shang Yang failed to show a passport to the innkeeper, he
was arrested and turned over to the royal guard. The new king
avenged his tutors' disfigurement by ordering a horrible death for
the prisoner: He was pulled to pieces by horse-drawn carriages.

Even so, the military machine of Qin that Shang Yang had
forged would produce his greatest legacy, the first Chinese empire.

4

THE FIRST CHINESE EMPIRE: THE QIN DYNASTY

221–207 B.C.

Qin Shihuangdi [Ch'in Shih-huang-ti]

We come now to one of the more familiar events of Chinese history, the founding of the first empire. The man responsible for this is also one of its best known personalities. He was the king of Qin, who conquered the Warring States and gave himself the title Shihuangdi, or First Great Emperor. (The *huang* in this title is not the same *huang* as in the title *Huangdi*, given the legendary Yellow Emperor; they are homonyms represented by two different Chinese characters.) The name of his empire, Qin, which is pronounced "Chin," is the root of the Western name China. (As we have seen, the Chinese call their country "Zhongguo," but they sometimes also refer to it by names meaning "All That Is Under Heaven" and "the Flowery Land.")

Shihuangdi was the great unifier, the builder of the Great Wall, the first emperor in historical times. The empire he created has lasted as a political and geographic entity for two thousand years, more than four times as long as the Roman Empire.

Who was this man? His birth is surrounded by legend and intrigue. He was born, it is said, with the nose of a scorpion, eyes like a vulture, and the voice of a wolf. He was merciless, with the heart of a tiger. His mother was the beautiful mistress of an

36

Qin Dynasty Empire (221–207 B.C.)

ambitious man named Lu Buwei [Lü Pu-wei] who was known for
his literary achievements. Lu came to the court of Qin and presented his mistress as a gift to the then crown prince of Qin. She
soon gave birth to a son, and historians have never settled the
question of whether the boy's father was Lu or the crown prince.
The crown prince had no such doubts. When, soon after, he
became king of Qin, he pronounced the baby his heir and made
Lu Buwei his prime minister. In 246 B.C., when the boy was only
thirteen, his royal father died, and the youth became king of Qin
with Lu as his regent and tutor.

Lu endorsed the strong central authority and tightly controlled
military force established a hundred years earlier by Shang Yang,
as well as the pattern of conquest begun when Shang Yang led
the Qin army to victory over the state of Wei. His pupil was a fast

37

learner: At the age of twenty-one he assumed full authority as king and banished Lu and the dowager queen because rumors of a continued liaison between them raised the issue of his dubious paternity. Lu later poisoned himself, but the dowager queen was eventually pardoned and brought back to court.

The king chose a new prime minister, Li Si [Li Ssu], a scholar and a Legalist in the tradition of Shang Yang who, through a combination of military force and betrayed alliances, helped the king to conquer all the rival Warring States. Since the fifth century B.C. these states had been fighting one another for just such control. The young king of Qin and his prime minister accomplished the task in seventeen years. In 221 B.C., the states were united and the king of Qin took the title Shihuangdi, declaring himself the "First Great Emperor" of a Qin dynasty which he imagined would rule forever over the Middle Kingdom. He was a man who conceived things on a grand scale. (He would have appreciated the efforts of his less successful contemporary, the great Carthaginian general Hannibal, who, in 218 B.C., invaded northern Italy by crossing the Alps with an army of men and elephants.)

Qin Shihuangdi did not trust his newly conquered enemies. His life had already been threatened by an assassination plot prior to his subjugation of the Warring States. In this instance, an envoy posing as a sympathizer to the king of Qin brought him a map showing the best route for the invasion of a state resisting Qin dominance. Hidden in the map was a dagger which the envoy drew and thrust at the king's heart. The king was too quick; he leaped aside as the dagger went into the wooden back of his throne. After this he had the palace gates lined with special magnetic metals for detection of concealed weapons.

As emperor, he took further precautions and ordered the kings of the conquered states to bring their courts west to live near his capital city, Xianyang [Hsien-yang] (north across the Wei River from present-day Xi'an), where he could keep an eye on them and where they would have no power base. Furthermore, he gathered all their metal armaments, melted them, and had them made into great bells and fifty-foot statues.

Shihuangdi's ruthless use of power inevitably earned him the criticism of the Confucian scholars, who quoted from the Five

Figure 14. *This is the most contemporary representation known of China's great unifier, Qin Shihuangdi. The scene illustrates an attempted assassination of the future emperor. On the left, the would-be assassin, hair flying, is held back by the royal physician. The dagger he has just hurled has cut off the monarch's sleeve and is lodged in the wooden throne back. Meanwhile, to the right of the throne, the emperor-to-be leaps to safety, holding high the jade circle, symbol of heaven; a guard rushes to his assistance, and the assailant's companion falls to the ground.* Rubbing from a second-century-A.D. stone relief, Wu family tombs, in Jiaxiang, Shandong province

Classics and the Four Books on the proper behavior of a ruler. They talked of the illustrious legendary trio, Yao, Shun, and Yu, whose first concern had been the welfare of their people, and recalling Shun's exemplary filial devotion, they admonished the emperor for banishing his mother. Such talk enraged the emperor, who asked his minister, Li Si, to come up with an answer to the critics. Li Si pointed out that if the emperor destroyed all records of these early rulers, no one could hold them up as models. History would then begin with the Qin dynasty. Shihuangdi would be free of criticism and could establish all the precedents for his heirs. Following his advice, Shihuangdi decreed that all books recording events of the past or moral example be burned. He specifically excepted books of divination, such as the *I-ching*, and of medicine, as these might help him either to predict the future or to stay in good health. Fortunately the order was carried out only in part because many devoted scholars hid books in walls or buried them in gardens, where some were discovered centuries later. Also, it is said, after Shihuangdi's death, some elderly scholars who knew the classics by heart set them down from memory. And so they have survived. Only the *Book of Music* disappeared forever.

Figure 15. Recent excavations near the Qin capital are the basis for this restored Qin palace of the fourth to third centuries B.C., near Xianyang. The walls of the first floor double as the earthen foundation for the two upper stories, which are built of wood. Courtesy of the China Institute in America

The emperor became obsessed with protecting his life and summoned scholar after scholar to court, ordering them to provide him with an elixir that would give him immortality. After many had failed to satisfy this demand, a fat old man came to the palace and announced that he knew where to find such an elixir. "Great Emperor," he said as he kneeled before the throne, "if you will bring together four hundred of your strongest young warriors, four hundred of your most beautiful maidens, and four hundred of the finest horses in the empire, and if you will gather into caskets your finest jewels and silk cloths and put all these young people, horses, and treasures onto your sturdiest ships, I will sail with them across the sea and present them as gifts to the king who lives on the islands and guards the elixir of immortality. He will be unable to refuse such an incomparable tribute and will accept your gifts in exchange for the elixir."

The emperor was delighted with this prospect and gave the man all that he asked for. The precious cargo sailed away to the East, and the emperor waited impatiently for the elixir. But he waited in vain; the old man was never seen again, and some say that he and his cargo settled on the Japanese islands, or perhaps in the South Seas. Shihuangdi revenged himself by burying alive over four hundred of the scholars who had been most vociferous in their criticisms of his rule and had failed him in his search for an elixir of immortality.

This fanatical approach to solving any and all difficulties often caused great grief, but there were instances when, in the long run, it brought great benefits to the Chinese. One example was the standardization of the written language. Before the unification of the empire, each state had developed slightly differing forms of the written characters. Shihuangdi ordered samples of these collected and used them to create a single set of characters that was then used throughout the empire. One set of characters is still used in China's written language today. There are many mutually unintelligible dialects but a common written language. The Mandarin-speaking resident of Beijing cannot understand his countryman from Guangzhou [Kuang-chou] (Canton), who speaks Cantonese, but they can write to each other and read the same newspapers, books, and posters. (Mandarin was originally the language of scholar-officials; today it has been made the official language throughout China, and children are being taught to speak as well as write it. They also learn their own local dialect.)

Another of Shihuangdi's unifying strategies was to make all cartwheels the same distance apart by specifying a uniform axle length. Thus, all wheel ruts in the dirt roads of his empire were the same, and his troops and produce could travel faster. (In modern times, railway gauges the world over posed the same problem until a standard was agreed upon.)

The best known of the first emperor's grand schemes was the Great Wall. This has become his and China's trademark. As early as the fifth century B.C., rammed earth walls had been used by the northernmost states of the Spring and Autumn period as defenses against the invasions of nomadic tribes. Qin Shihuangdi put an estimated 300,000 conscripts to work connecting these fortifications into a continuous wall, from the Pacific coast to what is now Gansu province, which would permanently delineate and defend the boundary between his empire and the nomadic tribes. So many of these laborers died on the job that their creation has been dubbed the world's longest graveyard. Shihuangdi supposedly specified that the wall be wide and strong enough for six horsemen to ride abreast along its top (six was his favorite number). The course of this original Great Wall has been changed many times as later dynasties found it necessary to relocate, rebuild, or extend their northern defenses. It is more accurate to refer to a chronological series of Great Walls rather than a single, consistently located structure dating from Qin Shihuangdi's time. The present

Figure 16. The Great Wall as rebuilt during the Ming dynasty (1368–1644) is featured in a nineteenth-century wood-block print from a Chinese gazetteer. Harvard-Yenching Library, Harvard University

wall is the reconstruction of the Ming dynasty (1368–1644); then, it was rebuilt along its present path, and much of its length—which is said to be currently either fifteen or twenty-five hundred miles long, depending on one's source—was refaced with stone masonry, and at strategic intervals, castlelike watchtowers were built. These watchtowers also served as quarters for troops, re-

Figure 17. After the Manchu conquest of China in 1644, the Great Wall (seen here in an early twentieth-century photograph) fell into disrepair, but today large sections have been restored and are scaled by millions from all corners of the earth. Library of Congress

placing smaller guard posts. Most visitors see a part of the Ming wall at Badaling, fifty miles north of Beijing, which has been restored in recent years.

Throughout long periods of China's history, and especially the Han and Ming dynasties, these Great Walls served their purpose. Troops garrisoned along them used smoke, fire, and flag signals to warn of invasion and call for reinforcements. However, during periods of internal disunity, the military presence as well as the walls themselves weakened or disappeared altogether, and the nomads not only crossed what was left but settled down in Chinese territories. There were three major waves of such nomadic infiltration. The first, during the third to sixth centuries, only affected North China; the other two resulted in the Mongolian and Manchu conquests of all China. (In the latter case, it was not the wall that failed so much as internal loyalties: A treacherous Ming general opened the principal eastern gate to the Manchu troops.)

When Shihuangdi realized that he must die, or at least leave the life of the living, he planned for his life among the dead on a

Figure 18. Six thousand life-size clay figures were buried in battle formation, ready to defend Qin Shihuangdi's life after death. New China Pictures Co.

characteristically grand scale. Seven hundred thousand laborers slaved on an elaborate burial complex northeast of Xi'an. They created six thousand life-size clay warriors, standing in battle formation. These warriors led life-size clay horses and held real metal and wooden weapons. Each soldier or officer wore the uniform of his rank and, most astounding of all, had individualized features, heights, and hairdos. This clay army was buried facing east, ready to defend the emperor's tomb from his recently conquered enemies.

Behind the clay army, a mile or so to the west, the actual tomb rose as an enormous tumulus. Inside it, supposedly, is a vast underground palace, the main room of which has a domed ceiling studded with gems representing stars, a floor designed to be a map of the empire with the rivers filled with flowing mercury and the emperor's body borne by a boat afloat the largest, the Yellow River. Protective mazes full of booby traps surround this chamber. How do we know all this? The artisans who built the tomb were buried alive inside so they would not reveal the plan of the tomb. But one of them escaped and, after fifty years in hiding, revealed the

Figure 19. Qin Shihuangdi's body is said to lie on a boat floating on a river of mercury under a domed gem-studded sky, all beneath this small mountain of a tumulus. An Kerin, New China Pictures Co.

secret of the tomb's location and design. There are some accounts that say the tomb was plundered shortly after the fall of the Qin, but we must wait for Chinese archeologists, who are now making plans for its excavation, to reveal the truth of such rumors and of the description that has come down to us.

The clay army was discovered by accident in 1973 when a peasant drilling a well in the fields covering it broke through into the pit containing the warriors. It has now been extensively excavated and made into an awesome display the size of a football field.

After Shihuangdi's death, his second son and designated heir was quickly toppled by the many rebellious factions that rose up to challenge him, and, in 207 B.C., a mere fourteen years after Shihuangdi's grand pronouncement that his rule would last for all eternity, the Qin dynasty ended. The concept of his empire, however—a unified country under one rule—has survived to the present through many changes of size, dynastic shifts, and foreign invasions.

5

THE HAN DYNASTY

206 B.C.–220 A.D.

The Han dynasty, established after the fall of the Qin, ruled China for four hundred years and is divided into two periods: the Western Han (capital at Chang'an, near Xi'an in the west, from 206 B.C. to 8 A.D.) and, after an eighteen-year interregnum, the Eastern Han (capital at Luoyang from 25 to 220 A.D.). The Han dynasty was the first of four great, long-lived native Chinese (as opposed to Mongol or Manchu) dynasties. The other three were the Tang, the Song, and the Ming.

Western Han Dynasty

206 B.C.–8 A.D.

Han Gaozu [Kao-tsu]

After the collapse of the Qin rule in 207 B.C., there was a period of anarchic rebellion as factions vied for the imperial throne. Finally the leader of one faction, known to posterity as Han Gaozu, emerged victorious and established the new Han dynasty. The name Han has been used ever since to differentiate the ethnic Chinese, now about 94 percent of the population, from the fifty

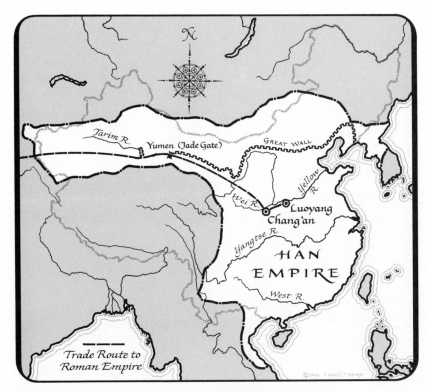

Han Dynasty Empire (206 B.C.–A.D. 220)

or so other ethnic groups—Mongolians, Tibetans, Miao, Uygurs, etc.—who form the remainder. And Gaozu?

That's not so simple. The names of Chinese emperors require brief explanation. Qin Shihuangdi, or First Great Emperor of Qin, took this title for himself while he was alive, and this is the name he goes by in history as well. However, beginning with the Han, emperors were known by a posthumous title composed of a glorifying adjective such as *high, martial,* or *great* (in Chinese *gao, wu,* and *tai* respectively) and either the word for emperor, *di,* or the word for ancestor, *zu.* Thus we have Gaozu ("High Progenitor"), Wudi ("Martial Emperor"), and so on. Sometimes, if an emperor had been considered a bad ruler, he was given a derogatory title such as the *Ai* in *Aidi,* which means "Pitiful Emperor." To prevent confusion in identifying the emperors of successive dynasties who acquired the same posthumous title, the dynasty name is added, as in *Han* (dynasty) *Gaozu,* or *Tang* (dynasty) *Gaozu.* In the thir-

47

Figure 20. A commoner led the successful rebellion against the Qin throne and became Han Gaozu, Grand Progenitor of the Han dynasty, which ruled the empire for over four hundred years. The Metropolitan Museum of Art, gift of Mrs. Edward S. Harkness, 1947

teenth century, under the Mongol rule, the Mongolian emperors took Chinese titles, but they are better known by their Mongolian names and titles, as in *Kublai* (name) *Khan* (title). Finally, with the Ming and Qing dynasty emperors, an emperor was known either by his posthumous Chinese title or by the title given to his reign. In the latter case, we refer, for instance, to the Kangxi emperor, *Kangxi* being the reign title. It is technically incorrect to say "Emperor Kangxi."

The original family and given names of an emperor were considered forbidden names; they could not be said aloud or written in documents, nor could they be taken by anyone during the emperor's lifetime. He was addressed by deferential terms referring to his exalted position, such as "Son of Heaven," "Your Myriad Years," or simply "Highness."

Han Gaozu started his career as Liu Bang [Liu Pang], a man of the people who became an official under the Qin emperor Shihuangdi. He was assigned the job of overseer to some of the slaves who worked to build Shihuangdi's tomb. But he broke rank, set the slaves free, and led them into the mountains, where they lived as outlaws and plotted rebellion. When Shihuangdi died, Liu Bang and his men gathered more followers and challenged the Qin throne. They were challenged in turn by another, more legitimate contender for the throne, a former Eastern Zhou general; after a bitter period of fighting, Liu Bang finally emerged triumphant. His success is attributed to his gift for gregarious but shrewd leadership. When he ascended the throne, he rejected the title emperor for himself, preferring the title king, and, as explained above, at his death in 195 B.C., he acquired the posthumous name Gaozu, "High Progenitor." The title is appropriate because his twelve-year rule, spent in continual fighting to hold the empire together, established the supremacy of the Han dynasty for an almost uninterrupted four hundred years.

Han Wudi [Wu-ti]

Wudi, or Martial Emperor, the sixth emperor of the Han dynasty, reigned from 141 to 87 B.C. His fifty-four-year reign, the longest of a native Chinese ruler (and exceeded by those of only two Manchu emperors, in the seventeenth and eighteenth centuries), was full of wide-ranging achievements. His ambitious and brilliant military strategies expanded the empire into most of the areas included in today's China. He extended the Great Wall as far as the Yumen ("the Jade Gate") in the west while making allies of many of the tribes beyond it. As an enlightened administrator, he had civil servants selected from the populace at large by means of examination questions he had made up by himself and passed on to the local officials who tested the candidates. Confucian scholars chosen in this way persuaded the emperor to make Confucian philosophy the state orthodoxy. In 124 B.C. they also persuaded him to establish a state university near the capital where the empire's ablest young men could study Confucian texts. After one year of study, the graduates were examined to determine whether they qualified for government service. This process was the precursor of the complex examination system that was to become institutionalized under later dynasties. Finally Wudi was a man of great culture whose court was filled with poets, musicians, dancers, and artists.

As a result of Han Wudi's expansionist policy, China came into contact with Western culture for the first time. In 139 B.C. his most famous general, Zhang Qian [Chang Ch'ien], set out with a small force to negotiate an alliance with a northwestern tribe against a common enemy, the Xiongnu [Hsiung-nu] (known to us as the Huns). Before he could reach his allies-to-be, Zhang Qian was captured by the Xiongnu and held prisoner for ten years. When he managed to escape, instead of returning home, he con-

Figure 21. The dress and hairstyle favored by women in the court of Han Wudi presumably resembled those of these glazed earthenware Han tomb figurines. The Metropolitan Museum of Art, Rogers Fund, 1910

tinued his search for the friendly tribes. They had moved west and were now fighting for possession of Bactria (part of present-day Afghanistan). This was a country that had been ruled by Greek kings ever since their ancestors, led by Alexander the Great in the fourth century B.C., had conquered it as part of the Persian Empire. Zhang Qian spent a year trying, unsuccessfully, to work out an alliance against the Xiongnu. He finally returned to China in 126 B.C. with two products unknown in China, walnuts and grapevines, and the even more important news that there were kingdoms in the West that were interested in trading with the Han empire and were particularly intrigued by silk. This was the first step in establishing the great Silk Road, over which trade between China and the Mediterranean flourished under later Han emperors and again during the Tang dynasty (618–907).

Han Wudi, who was a poet as well, wrote the following lines as he embarked for an official expedition on his state barge:

> *Autumn wind rises: white clouds fly.*
> *Grass and trees wither: geese go south.*
> *Orchids all in bloom: chrysanthemums smell sweet.*
> *I think of my lovely lady: I can never forget.*
> *Floating-pagoda boat crossed Fen River.*
> *Across the mid-stream white waves rise;*
> *A flute and drum keep time to the sound of the*
>   *rowers' song;*
> *Amidst revel and feasting, sad thoughts come;*
> *Youth's years how few! Age how sure!*[1]

"Age how sure!" Writing poetry was for him one way of coping with his preoccupation with mortality. Searching for an elixir of youth was another. Han Wudi, like Qin Shihuangdi before him and many emperors after him, was obsessed with the idea of obtaining such an elixir and asked the aid of Daoist sages, who practiced alchemy in their search for the dao, or path, to spiritual

---

1. Han Wudi, in Arthur Waley, trans., *Translations from the Chinese* (New York: Alfred A. Knopf, 1945), 36.

unity with nature. Once, when one of these presented the emperor with a specially brewed potion, Wudi's favorite minister, a man of great wit and presumption, stepped up and took the potion from the Daoist and drank it himself. The emperor was beside himself with rage and condemned the minister to death.

"If the potion was genuine," exclaimed the minister, "you cannot kill me, whereas if it was not, what harm has been done?"

This quick-witted reply saved the minister his life, but it did not stop Wudi and his successors from continuing their search for immortality. The historical records indicate that so-called elixirs of life were often lethal potions that occasionally even killed an emperor.

The records of alchemists list sulphur and saltpeter as two of the ingredients regarded as especially promising. When some unknown eighth-century experimenter mixed them with charcoal, he discovered "fire medicine." We call it gunpowder. So much for immortality.

Sima Qian [Ssu-ma Ch'ien]

Much of the history we have covered so far is known through the writings of Sima Qian (145–90 B.C.), who is regarded as the Chinese Herodotus. He came from a family of official court historians and inherited from his father, during the reign of Han Wudi, the ambitious task of writing an updated version of his country's history. While he worked on this, one of the emperor's generals was captured alive in a battle with the Xiongnu. The emperor pronounced the general a traitor because he had neither fought to his death nor sought escape in suicide; the general's family were all sentenced to death. Sima Qian dared to defend the general's actions and was himself pronounced a traitor; given the choice of death or castration, he chose the latter so that he might honor the pledge made to his dying father to complete the great history. The result is the renowned *Records of the Historian*, which has become the primary source for traditional Chinese history, from the earliest legendary rulers to the Western Han dynasty.

Wang Mang

By 9 A.D., eleven Han emperors had ruled from Chang'an and true to tradition, this succession became increasingly corrupt and self-indulgent. Then a controversial figure stepped in and tried to reform the government and the organization of society. This was Wang Mang, a maternal uncle to one of the last Western Han emperors, and thus not a member of the Han dynasty. He took the throne by coup d'état in the ninth year of the Christian era and announced the beginning of the Xin [Hsin] ("New") dynasty, of which he was the first and only ruler.

Wang Mang is best remembered as a great reformer. He advocated redistribution of land, taxation of slave owners (his original hope of freeing slaves proved unrealistic), and replacing gold coins with bronze (the imperial treasury thereby acquired a vast hoard of gold). However, corrupt civil servants sabotaged his reforms, and peasants and landowners alike found the disruption of the status quo too unsettling. Secret societies, with names such as the Red Eyebrows and the Green Woodsman, describing either distinguishing facial features or places of origin, rose in rebellion and then joined forces with the recently deposed Han.

After a fourteen-year reign, Wang Mang was captured by his adversaries and beheaded. Though many of his reforms did eventually become guidelines for later Chinese rulers, historians view the man himself either as an important reformer or an ambitious usurper.

Eastern Han Dynasty
25–220

Two years after Wang Mang's death, a cousin of the former Western Han emperor became leader of the revived Han dynasty, which, in 25 A.D., became known as the Eastern Han because the capital had been relocated at Luoyang. The Eastern Han had fourteen emperors and ruled until 220 A.D. During this two-century period, the contacts between East and West, initiated under Han Wudi, expanded into a flourishing trade between the Eastern Han empire and the Roman Empire, then in its full glory. The first great Silk Road, traveled by caravans loaded with exotica from both ends, went from Luoyang, across Central Asia and the Middle East, to the Mediterranean. Chinese silk was an exclusive, glamorous product, for which the Romans were insatiable customers, spending so much of their money on it that it had to be rationed in order to stop the eastward flow of cash. The coin that the Romans gave their silk dealers was transformed many times over by middlemen until it reached the Chinese in the form of horses, cattle, nuts, and seeds.

There are two major figures whose lives reflect, on the one hand, the expansionist ambitions of the Eastern Han, and on the other, the intellectual concerns of the court elite; they happen to be brother and sister, Ban Chao and Ban Zhao. (In Chinese the surname precedes the given name.)

Ban Chao [Pan Ch'ao]

Ban Chao (32–102) was one of China's greatest generals and a member of a family of illustrious scholars. In 73 A.D. he began the reconquest of the Tarim River basin in Central Asia (present-day Xinjiang Uygur province). Since the second century B.C., when Han Wudi had first brought this area into the empire, the constant attacks of the Xiongnu and other tribes had all but abolished Han control there. Ban Chao reinstated Chinese rule, ingeniously persuading one tribal faction to subdue another in the name of the emperor. In 91 A.D. he was made governor-general of the Western Territories. (The Xiongnu, once again frustrated in their attempts to invade China, moved west across Asia; eventually, in the fifth century, led by the famous Attila, they swept into the faltering Roman Empire and precipitated its death throes.)

At the end of the first century A.D., Ban Chao led a large expedition to the Caspian Sea, almost four thousand miles from Luoyang. From there he sent an envoy to the Roman Empire. In this case, all roads did not lead to Rome. Ban Chao's deputy was stopped at the northeastern shore of the Persian Gulf by the tales of Parthian sailors who, one suspects, did not want to be done out of their lucrative role as middlemen on the silk route. The sailors warned the Chinese that the Persian Gulf was an uncharted, treacherous sea that could take three years to cross and that many of those who had tried had turned back in homesick desperation. The deputy returned to Ban Chao with this disappointing report; no further attempts were made to go to Rome, and Ban Chao returned to China in 102.

Within a hundred years, however, Arabs and Romans reached China; the Arabs came by sea to Guangzhou in 147 and an ambassador of the Roman emperor Marcus Aurelius came to Luoyang in 166. This latter brought African exotica with him—rhinoceros horn and ivory tusks—as gifts for the Eastern Han emperor.

Ban Zhao [Pan Chao]

While Ban Chao was busy keeping things in order on the western frontier, his sister Ban Zhao (49–120) was becoming China's most famous woman scholar, working with her father and brother Ban Gu on the history of the earlier, or Western, Han dynasty. Ban Gu [Pan Ku] (32–92) is considered the main author, but after he and his father died, Ban Zhao completed the opus. The *History of the Former Han Dynasty*, the first self-contained history of a single dynastic period, became the model copied by authors of the histories of succeeding dynasties.

How did Ban Zhao achieve such scholarship, so unusual for a woman of her day? She dutifully married at fourteen, but her husband died soon after the marriage; she returned to the paternal home, where she was encouraged to devote herself to scholarship with her father and brother. While she worked on the Han history, she also wrote poetry and treatises advocating, among other things, education for women (which, however, was not taken seriously in China until 1949). Ban Zhao tried to teach the ladies of the Eastern Han court, but according to the nineteenth-century inscription seen on figure 22, "they were like stones" and were unable to learn from the history that she and her family had written.

Figure 22. A traditional representation of Ban Zhao, painted on a nineteenth-century ceramic jar, shows her trying to teach history to the illiterate ladies of the Eastern Han court.

The remarkable lives of Ban Chao and Ban Zhao speak not only for an unusual family but also for the scope of the Eastern Han world. This world, so rich in territories and culture, was coming to an end. The empire had spread too far to be managed by later Han rulers, men who had become increasingly weak and ineffectual. In 220 A.D., four hundred years of Han supremacy ended with the forced resignation of the last Eastern Han emperor. Years of turmoil had led to this, turmoil particularly fostered by three different groups, as we shall see.

No single destructive queen or nomadic invasion was to blame this time. Rather, there was first the quick succession of young emperors who followed one another to early and suspicious deaths. Second, there were the generals and the court eunuchs vying for the power behind the throne at the expense of the bureaucratic administrators. Eunuchs had been present in Chinese court life since at least the eighth century B.C. Their ostensible job, as guardians of the imperial wives and concubines, was to ensure the purity of royal lineage. However, these men of low social origins, who frequently achieved their status through self-mutilation, were the emperor's most loyal allies. During the Eastern Han period, they were intimates of the imperial household, and their influence, though unofficial, rivaled that of the appointed scholar-officials.

The adopted son of a eunuch, Cao Cao [Ts'ao Ts'ao], became a powerful and infamous general. Finally, a third group, the peasants, challenged both of the others. They joined in a society called the Yellow Turbans and rebelled against oppressive landlords. Cao Cao and rival generals fought both each other and the Yellow Turbans while emperor after emperor died young. Ultimately, Cao Cao forced the resignation of the last emperor and tried to claim the empire for himself. But it was too late, and the empire disintegrated.

Earlier, in the midst of the chaos, one of Cao Cao's rivals had ordered the destruction of the capital city of Luoyang. Cao Cao's son, a native of Luoyang and a poet, mourned his lost home in verse. His poem can serve here as an epitaph for the fallen empire:

> *I climb to the ridge of Pei Mang Mountain*
> *And look down on the city of Lo-yang.*
> *In Lo-yang how still it is!*
> *Palaces and houses all burnt to ashes.*
> *Walls and fences all broken and gaping,*
> *Thorns and brambles shooting up to the sky.*
> *I do not see the old-men:*
> *I only see the new young men.*
> *I turn aside, for the straight road is lost:*
> *The fields are overgrown and will never be ploughed again.*
> *I have been away such a long time*
> *That I do not know which street is which.*
> *How sad and ugly the empty moors are!*
> *A thousand miles without the smoke of a chimney.*
> *I think of the house I lived in all those years:*
> *I am heart-tied and cannot speak.*[2]

2. Cao Zhi, ibid., 64.

6

THE SECOND PERIOD
OF DISUNITY

220–589

A fter the collapse of the Han empire in 220, the map of China
becomes a giant kaleidoscope where political units shift rest-
lessly in the struggle for ascendancy during the next three
centuries. A brief summary will make apparent the complex nature
of this period.

First, the Han empire broke into the Three Kingdoms—Wei,
Shu, and Wu—which lasted from 220 to 265. This division was
as much geographic as political: The kingdom of Wei included
the Yellow River basin and the plateaus of the north, that of Shu,
the western fertile basins of four rivers now called Sichuan [Ssu-
ch'uan] ("Four Rivers") province, and the third, Wu, the still
sparsely populated Yangtse River basin in the south. Then, in
265, the kingdom of Wei absorbed the kingdom of Shu and this
new unit took the name of the Western Jin dynasty. In 280, the
kingdom of Wu was also annexed by the Western Jin and, for a
brief interlude, until 316, the empire was reunited.

Early in the fourth century, however, even before the close of
the Western Jin tenure, nomadic tribes, known in Chinese histories
as those of the "five barbarians," pushed down from the north and
northwest and began to settle on the plains and plateaus south of
the Great Wall. By 316, they had taken North China away from

The Three Kingdoms (220–265)

the Western Jin and had created the first of a series of small
kingdoms (collectively known as the Sixteen Kingdoms, 316–420)
over which they fought among themselves incessantly. The leaders
of these nomads, eager to adopt Chinese ways, gave their dominions names from the Chinese past, assumed dynastic titles, and
intermarried with the Chinese. Meanwhile, in 317 in South China,
members of the family that had founded the Western Jin dynasty
established the Eastern Jin dynasty with a capital in Nanjing
[Nanking]. The north-south boundary was challenged when the
ambitious ruler of one of the Sixteen Kingdoms, the Former Qin,
set out in 383 to conquer South China, but his enormous army
was so roundly defeated by the much smaller and more disciplined
Eastern Jin force that for the next two centuries South China was
left to the Chinese. Now followed a period, from 420 to 589,

59

referred to as the Northern and Southern Dynasties. During this time the north was ruled by the descendants of the five barbarian tribes who now took the dynastic names of Northern, Eastern and Western Wei, the Northern Zhou, and the Northern Qi. In the south, the Eastern Jin dynasty was succeeded by the Song, Qi, Liang, and Chen dynasties.

If the political history of this time, with its many names, dates, and territorial divisions, is enough to make the most interested of Westerners give up hope of ever getting Chinese history straight, this very clash of dynasties was also the source of great cultural diversity, enrichment, and inspiration. For the Chinese of later centuries, the earlier part of this period, that of the Three Kingdoms, is one full of epic drama and heroes. It gave its name to a famous Chinese saga, *The Romance of the Three Kingdoms* (actually written down in the late fourteenth century), which is comparable to the English tales of King Arthur and the Knights of the Round Table. The stories in the Chinese book are based on folklore but are largely supported by the separate historical records of the Three Kingdoms. Both are full of characters well known to every Chinese. The most famous of all these is the godlike Zhugeliang, the scholar-statesman-strategist whose genius guided the fortunes of his friend, Liu Bei, founder of the Kingdom of Shu.

Zhugeliang [Chu Ko-liang]

During the last years of the Han rule, a distant and impoverished cousin of the emperor eked out a living making straw sandals for travelers whose feet grew sore from the rough roads. His name was Liu Bei [Liu Pei]. At this time, the Yellow Turban revolt was gaining in force, and a call went out for volunteers to fight against the rebels. Liu Bei decided to become a soldier.

He fought under one general after another but discovered that all were ready to betray the house of Han, of which he was a member. So, having risen in rank and influence, he struck out on his own to defend the throne. He needed a good adviser, however, and was told of Zhugeliang, a man of extraordinary abilities, a great scholar, who lived in seclusion in a reed hut on a sacred mountain and was known as Master Sleeping Dragon. Twice Liu

Figure 23. The revered scholar-statesman Zhugeliang was one of the heroes of the Three King-doms period. His sangfroid in the face of danger is legendary.

Bei went with gifts to the reed hut, but the master was away. The third time, he found him at home and begged him to help plan a strategy by which order could be restored under Han rule. Zhu-geliang was willing to discuss a plan but was reluctant to leave his peaceful life in the mountains. At last he was persuaded and, in the service of Liu Bei, and later his son, became a central participant in the ferocious struggles that accompanied the breakup of Han rule into the Three Kingdoms. These struggles continued as each kingdom tried to dominate the other two.

Of all the wonderful stories about Zhugeliang, one especially captures the imagination. Throughout his long career, Zhugeliang's goal was reunification of the empire. He sought the definitive victory of the army of Shu, the kingdom created and ruled by Liu Bei and his sons, over that of Wei, the northern kingdom, founded by Cao Cao and his sons.

In one encounter, Zhugeliang sent a small advance army to meet its enemy counterpart. This was a mistake, for the enemy greatly outnumbered the Shu force and quickly finished them off. When word of this reached Zhugeliang's main army, the soldiers panicked, leaving their leader and three loyal companions to flee to a nearby fortified city.

Meanwhile the general of the enemy army, a man whose brilliance and reputation all but equaled Zhugeliang's, led his men toward this city. He heard the sound of music and singing coming from its walls and saw that the gates were wide open, with not a soldier in sight. The general looked up to see Zhugeliang dressed in finery, seated in the gate tower, playing away on a zither and singing with all the joy of a man who hasn't a care in the world. The general halted his army and considered the meaning of this strange scene.

"Surely this is a ruse," he thought. "Although not a soldier is to be seen on the ramparts nor in the gates, Zhugeliang sings too happily. He has always been more dangerous after a defeat than at the start of battle, and this time he has laid a trap and he waits for us to fall in. We will not go on."

To the dismay and consternation of his men, the general turned and retreated; Zhugeliang only sang louder than ever. The city fathers wondered at such daring but Zhugeliang answered them: "There was no daring, for the alternative was death."

As we have seen, the Three Kingdoms were briefly united under the Western Jin, but then came three centuries of political divisions and disruptions. The rise of Buddhism was the great cultural development of this time. The spread of this great religion in China occurred at about the same time as that of Christianity in the West. While the latter was certainly encouraged by Constantine's granting legal sanction to Christian worship in his Roman (later, Byzantine) Empire in 313, Buddhism's acceptance into China came in a more roundabout way.

The earliest mention of Buddhism in China is the story of an Eastern Han emperor, who, in 67 A.D., was said to have dreamed of a haloed figure. When his counselors told him that it must have been the Buddha, of whom they had heard, the emperor sent an envoy to India who eventually returned with two Indian Buddhist monks. What is certain is that Chinese versions of Indian Buddhist texts began to appear in the second century A.D. From these a growing number of Chinese learned the story of the Indian prince Gautama who, in the sixth century B.C., gave up all his earthly possessions to live as a wanderer, seeking enlightenment and freedom from the sufferings of the world of desire. Through his meditations, he achieved the state of perfect detachment—Nirvana—and became the Buddha. In translation this story, greatly simplified here, acquired Chinese attributes; Daoist terms were used to signify enlightenment, Nirvana, and immortality. By the fifth and sixth centuries, Chinese of the Southern Dynasties, who

Figure 24. Buddhism first received official sanction in the Northern Dynasties of the fourth and fifth centuries. The earliest examples of Chinese Buddhist art, such as this gilded bronze standing Buddha, are of this period. The Metropolitan Museum of Art, Kennedy Fund, 1926

had discovered through the upheavals of the previous two centuries that they could not rely on Confucian prescriptions for social harmony, were eager to retire to monastic communities and live out a life in meditation. These Buddhist centers in South China were not associated with any central government sanction. In contrast, in North China the recently Sinicized leaders of the Northern Dynasties saw in Buddhism a way of unifying their diverse subjects and, at the end of the fifth century, gave it official sanction and patronage.

In Central Asia there had been a long tradition of building Buddhist cave shrines and, from the fourth to the sixth centuries, this activity spread to North China. Under supervision of the Northern dynasts, large numbers of their populace devoted their energies to building great complexes of caves decorated with sculpture—often monumental in scale—and wall paintings illustrating the life of the Buddha. These sanctuaries helped to enlighten the illiterate devotee in much the same way that the mosaics and frescoes in early Christian churches helped spread the teachings of Christ. (See appendix II under Buddhist Art.)

Many of the Chinese Buddhist sculptures seen in museums in

the West today date from the Northern Dynasties and speak to us of the devotion of those who produced these serene, elegantly draped figures.

Bodhidharma

During the fourth, fifth, and sixth centuries, many Indian Buddhist monks came to China to teach and establish monasteries. They traveled either through the mountains and deserts of Central Asia or by sea, sailing around Southeast Asia. The most famous of these was Bodhidharma, who came by sea to the coast of South China in the sixth century and spent time at the court of a Southern Liang ruler. After instructing the Chinese emperor of the time, he crossed the Yangtse River on two reeds, so the legend goes, and carried his teachings to the Northern Wei ruler. He was renowned for his ability to meditate for days, months, even years. Another part of the legend tells the story of Bodhidharma and the origin of ritual tea drinking among Buddhists.

One day, as Bodhidharma sat meditating, he fell asleep. When he awoke, he was so angry that he tore off his eyelids and threw them on the ground.

"Now I shall never fall asleep again!" he cried.

The next day he returned to continue his meditation. At the spot where he had thrown his eyelids were two small bushes covered with tiny leaves, tea leaves. He picked off some of these and brewed them in boiling water and drank the potion. Suddenly he felt more awake than ever and continued his meditation without fatigue.

Bodhidharma's example, and that of others like him, was so persuasive that Buddhism became the most widespread religion not only in China, but in all of Asia.

By the end of the sixth century, Northern and Southern Dynasties were in disarray; a Buddhist scholar-statesman saw an opportunity to unify them and so brought the second age of empire to the Middle Kingdom.

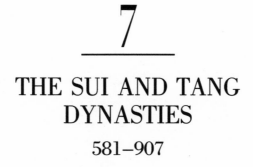

THE SUI AND TANG DYNASTIES

581–907

At the end of the sixth century, after more than three hundred years of division, the Chinese empire was reunited. The pattern of events following the first unification, when the Qin shaped an empire to rule it for only fourteen years, after which the long-lived Han dynasty kept it intact for four hundred more, repeated itself. The Sui rule (581–618) lasted through only two emperors and was followed by almost three hundred years of Tang [T'ang] rule (618–907). The Tang dynasty brought to China her great golden age of culture.

Sui Wendi [Sui Wen-ti]

The man who founded the Sui dynasty is known to posterity as Sui Wendi, or Sui Learned Emperor. He was brought up by a Buddhist nun who encouraged him to study and meditate. As the young duke of Sui, he used his learning in the service of an ambitious life of action. In 581 he usurped the throne of a Northern Zhou ruler and declared the start of the Sui dynasty. By 589, he had overcome the rest of the Northern and Southern Dynasties and reunited the Chinese empire.

Sui Wendi built a new capital city at Chang'an, near the site

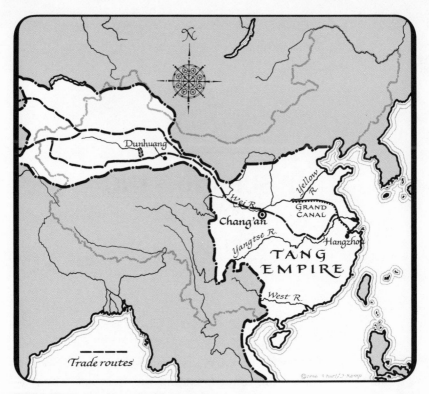

Tang Dynasty Empire (618–907)

of the old Western Han capital, and began construction of a Grand Canal, over which the produce grown in the fertile southern areas, around the lower Yangtse River, could easily be brought to the capital in the west. This canal required a labor force even more immense than that used by Qin Shihuangdi to build the Great Wall. Over five million conscripts, including women and children, were supervised by fifty thousand police, who stood over them with whips and chains. The result was a water system for communication and transportation that united the empire more securely than ever before.

The Sui Grand Canal has been replaced by alternate waterways constructed under later dynasties, but another example of the Sui genius for construction is still in use today. This is the famous Zhaozhou [Chao-chou] Bridge, in Hebei province, south of Beijing. Built at the start of the sixth century, it is a feat of extraordinary engineering; its single arch of forty meters, with upper side arches

66

隋文帝真像

帝名堅楊姓華陰人在位二十四年

Figure 25. A young Buddhist nobleman, later known as Sui Wendi, reunified China by 589 and started building the first Grand Canal. The Metropolitan Museum of Art, gift of Mrs. Edward S. Harkness, 1947

for both support and water passage, all built of limestone blocks, has withstood the floods of over thirteen centuries. Similar construction appeared only seven hundred years later in Europe.

Sui Yangdi [Sui Yang-ti]

In 605 Sui Wendi was purportedly killed by his son, who became the second and last Sui emperor. Yangdi's reputation begins with patricide and proceeds from there; he is considered one of the most evil of Chinese emperors.

Figure 26. Sui Yangdi, second and last Sui emperor, is accused by historians of patricide. Here (black-robed figure, left) he walks ceremoniously behind his father. The two pairs of attendants are intentionally smaller in scale out of deference to the imperial figures. This scene is from The Thirteen Emperors, *a seventh-century-A.D. hand scroll.* Courtesy of the Museum of Fine Arts, Boston, Denman Waldo Ross Collection

Under his reign, the conscription of workers for canal building from the population at large continued. The emperor rode up and down the new waterways aboard "dragon boats" filled with carousing courtiers and concubines, oblivious to the masses who slaved at his expense. He had grandiose plans for the conquest of the Korean peninsula and sent off three successive armies to realize this ambition. All three expeditions failed; thousands of Chinese soldiers died, and the imperial treasury went bankrupt.

Sui Yangdi retired from the capital to an eastern city, where he tried to forget his failures in a life of Buddhist meditation. One day, as he went to his ritual baths accompanied by his favorite son, one of his own bodyguards attacked him. The traitor swung his sword and lopped off the son's head. The horrified emperor, whose robes were spattered with blood, cried for mercy.

"Do not cut off my head! If you cut off my head, I can never be reborn! I can never reach Nirvana!"

The guard was touched. He strangled Yangdi first and then beheaded him.

The empire, reunited only nineteen years before, almost fell apart again, but a brilliant young aristocrat, Li Shimin, son of the Count of Tang, held it together while, with a devoted following of sixty thousand soldiers, he defeated all contenders to the throne in Chang'an. In 618 Li Shimin made his father the first emperor of the new Tang dynasty. He was given the same posthumous title as the first Han emperor, Gaozu, or High Progenitor, a signal that this new dynasty heralded a second glorious age of empire. Tang rule lasted until 907 and saw twenty emperors and one empress.

Tang Taizong [T'ang T'ai-tsung]

Taizong ("Grand Ancestor") is the posthumous title given to the brilliant Li Shimin, who succeeded his father as second Tang emperor. Since he had put his father on the throne, we might assume that he clearly deserved to inherit it, but Chinese history is never this simple. The father, while still emperor, resented the son's popularity and tried, with the help of Li Shimin's brothers, to poison him. Li Shimin was saved by an antidote. After two more attempts on his life, Li Shimin killed his brothers and their sons, forced his father to abdicate, and took control of the new empire. He reigned for twenty-three years, from 626 to 649, and died in his palace at the age of fifty-three.

Tang Taizong is remembered as one of the greatest of Chinese emperors, and despite the ruthless dispatch of his brothers and nephews, he was an exceptionally tolerant ruler. He was helped by his empress, a lady whose devotion to her husband was matched by her wit. A well-known story illustrates their partnership.

One day, when the emperor's favorite minister dared to criticize him, Taizong flew into a rage and vowed to have the minister killed. The empress went to her chambers, put on her ceremonial robes, and returned to her husband. She congratulated him on his good fortune.

"What is this all about?" inquired the emperor.

"Is it not said that only the wisest of rulers have honest coun-

Figure 27. Tang Taizong is considered one of the ablest and most tolerant of all Chinese emperors. His hat is designed to accommodate a topknot. The Metropolitan Museum of Art, gift of Mrs. Edward S. Harkness, 1947

selors?" she asked. "I congratulate you for your wisdom in having such a fine minister by your side."

The emperor forgave his minister and, like the great legendary Yao, learned to listen with an open mind.

Tang Taizong expanded the Tang empire into Central Asia, following the examples of Han Wudi and the Eastern Han general Ban Chao. A revived trade route brought riches to Chang'an from Europe, the Middle East, and India. Chang'an under the Tang was the most cosmopolitan city of the world in its day, a center for both international commerce and religious exchange between Confucians, Daoists, Buddhists, Moslems, and Christians. Its site is that of today's Xi'an, but its area was more than twice that of the present city. A famous Chinese Buddhist monk, Xuanzhuang [Hsüan-tsang], undertook an arduous sixteen-year pilgrimage (629–645) across deserts and mountain ranges to India's centers of Buddhism. (The story of this journey inspired the well-known comic allegory *Journey to the West*, also called *Monkey*, written in the sixteenth century by the scholar Wu Chengen [Wu Ch'eng-en]. The hero of this folk novel is not the pilgrim but his troublesome companion, the Monkey King.) Xuanzhuang brought back to Chang'an a wealth of new philosophical ideas and encyclopedic information about the terrains he had crossed in his travels. Tang Taizong delighted in discoursing with him and built him a retreat in which he could translate the Buddhist texts and write an account of his travels. This was the Great Goose Pagoda, a towering structure which can still be visited in Xi'an.

Though the emperor was fascinated by Buddhism, he main-

Ancient Sites in Xi'an Area

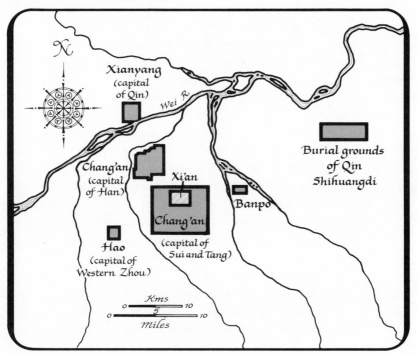

tained Confucianism as the official state doctrine. He decreed that throughout the empire temples to Confucius be built adjacent to schools for the training of Confucian scholar-officials. The use of examinations for selecting the best men for government service, originated by Han Wudi, was institutionalized, and this system became the source of the Chinese meritocracy—a ruling class chosen on the basis of education rather than aristocratic birthright. The system was extended at the end of the seventh century, under the empress Wu.

Empress Wuze Tian [Wu-tse T'ien]

The empress Wu (her full title is Wu, Equal of Heaven), who reigned from 690 to 705, was the only woman in Chinese history to call herself Son of Heaven, to assume the imperial dragon robes, and to carry out the rituals followed by her male counterparts. By all accounts, she was an extraordinary woman.

Empress Wu entered court life as a concubine in the harem of Tang Taizong at age thirteen. At his death, she retired with the rest of his concubines to a Buddhist nunnery but was soon asked by the succeeding emperor's wife to come divert the new emperor from the charms of his young concubine. It was not long before the future empress Wu had become the emperor's favorite and had arranged for the torture and eventual death of both the young concubine and the empress. The emperor became her puppet; after his death, she deposed his heir, took the throne herself, and announced the start of a new Zhou [Chou] dynasty. She found support among Buddhist monks whose power and influence had increased considerably since the beginning of the Tang dynasty. They even backed her spurious claim that she was the reincarnation of a Buddhist divinity, the Maitreya, whose arrival in the form of an emperor's concubine—so she said—had been predicted.

She maintained her position through a combination of forceful intelligence and cruelty. All who challenged her, and there were many, were rounded up and either banished or put to death. However, at a time when nomadic tribes were once again attacking the northern borders, her generals not only held them at bay but carried out the conquest of the Korean peninsula. Within the

Figure 28. The empress Wu in a traditional representation.

武
后

empire, she saw to the systematic use of the examination system and took the innovative step of starting programs to educate women for civil service. Only in her eighties was she forced to step aside by court conspirators who surprised her in her bed at night and demanded her abdication. She died soon afterward, at the age of eighty-two, and imperial power reverted to the Tang dynasty. In Chinese histories she is often condemned as a wicked woman who held the throne by killing her own sons (which she did) and playing favorites with Buddhist monks. Begrudging credit is given her, however, for her able administration of the empire. To some degree such accounts reflect the bias of misogynistic Confucian historians, for if we compare her rule with those of countless of her male peers, we discover that while she was just as ruthless, she was a lot more effective than many of them.

(It is pertinent to note here that the status of women, never high in the Confucian order, suffered a severe setback sometime during the next two centuries when Chinese women began to bind their feet. There are no illustrations of bound feet dated earlier than the tenth century, but since it was widespread among the upper classes during the Song dynasty, it is likely that it was customary during the late Tang era. The women dancers of the late Tang era bound their feet for dancing and are cited as the originators of the practice. They were copied by concubines seeking to charm the emperors, and the custom spread from there. Eventually only women with bound feet could hope to marry at

Figure 29. The game of polo came to China from Central Asia during the Tang dynasty. Women, who did not practice foot-binding until the end of the Tang era, played as well as men. These glazed earthenware figures, found in a Tang tomb, represent a male and female player. The Metropolitan Museum of Art, Rogers Fund, 1910

all, let alone marry well. By the nineteenth century, Chinese women of all classes had bound feet, and even Manchu women, who were forbidden by Qing law to bind their feet, nonetheless took up the practice. Girls' feet were bound, starting at age four. Ten years later, their feet would be three-inch knobs, called "golden lilies," and their mincing steps would produce a hip-swaying gait that was considered especially alluring. The pain, which was excruciating during childhood, continued to a lesser degree throughout a woman's life.)

Tang Xuanzong [T'ang Hsüan-tsung]

A grandson of the empress Wu, Tang Xuanzong, or Mysterious Ancestor (also known as Ming Huang, or Enlightened Emperor), took the throne after her first two successors had rather shakily held things together, and his long reign (713–756) saw both the glorious flowering of Chinese culture and the onset of the Tang decline. He brought to court three of the greatest of Chinese poets, Li Bai, Du Fu, and Wang Wei. Wang Wei was also a revered painter and is considered the father of the grand tradition of Chinese landscape painting (see pages 181–183).

For the first half of his reign, Xuanzong, who was a brilliant administrator and strategist, brought political stability to the empire and its borders. He also discouraged luxurious living while encouraging the arts at festivals of music, dance, and poetry both at court and throughout the empire.

Then, in the middle of his reign, as he was getting on in years, his eye fell on Yang Yuhuan ("Jade Circlet"). She was the beautiful wife of his eighteenth son—and the lady often referred to as the fourth great beauty of Chinese history (see end of chapter 2). The emperor fell hopelessly in love. The lady was sent briefly, as a divorce procedure, to a nunnery and then brought back to court to become the emperor's favorite concubine. Before long she received the title by which she is best known, Yang Guifei [Yang Kuei-fei] ("Yang, Imperial Concubine of Highest Order"). Yang Guifei was not only beautiful but talented in music and dance and would perform, with, we must suppose, unbound feet, at court soirées as the emperor beat the drum. As the favorite, she was entitled to such self-indulgences as fresh lichees brought daily for her breakfast from Guangzhou province, over five hundred miles away. She and the emperor swore never to part.

There was in the court at this time a general, An Lushan, a Turk who had been a slave. He was a robust, jovial man who amused Yang Guifei so much that she made him her protégé. The emperor favored An Lushan with the governorship of a border province; it was not a wise move. From this distance, An Lushan plotted revolt while the emperor, beguiled by his lady love, paid no attention to rumors of the new governor's treachery. When An Lushan attacked the capital, the emperor, his court, and his armies were caught by surprise and fled. The emperor ordered his forces to prepare for battle. The soldiers refused to obey his command until Yang Guifei, whom they considered both the cause of the emperor's negligence and an ally of An Lushan, was put to death. Poor Xuanzong had no choice. The most romantic version of this tale ends with Xuanzong sending Yang Guifei the silken cord with which she hung herself from a pear tree near the hot springs outside of Chang'an. Xuanzong gave up his throne to his son and retired

Figure 30. The irresistible Yang Guifei is helped to her saddle as the adoring emperor Tang Xuanzong reins in his impatient mount in this Yuan dynasty hand scroll. Courtesy of the Freer Gallery of Art, Smithsonian Institution, Washington, D.C.

to mourn his lost love. A poem of the period records the old emperor's grief:

> *On his return the garden was unaltered*
> *With its lotus and its willows;*
> *The lotus recalled her face*
> *The willows her eyebrows,*
> *And at the sight of these he could not hold back his*
> *tears.*[1]

An Lushan was assassinated by his own son and, although the rebellion he started officially ended six years later, in 763, it led to a prolonged era of internal strife that depleted the population and the imperial treasury. By the mid-ninth century, the Tang emperors lost effective control of the military commanders in charge of separate regions within the empire, and, in the beginning of the tenth century, Tang rule came to an end while these strongmen divided the empire among themselves.

1. Bai Juyi [Po Chü-i] in Hilda Hookham, *A Short History of China* (London: Longmans, Green and Co. Ltd, 1969), 107.

Li Bai [Li Po]

Li Bai (also pronounced Li Bo) (701–762) is thought to have been born in Central Asia. He is often referred to by his nickname, Zhe Xian ("Banished Immortal"), a Daoist term for those who have misbehaved in heaven and are sent to earth for a while. Such persons are recognizable because they defy all social conventions; Li Bai fulfilled this role admirably. He was a negligent husband and father; he enjoyed getting drunk with his fellow poets, a group that was later called the Eight Immortals of the Wine Cup. But his drunken, impertinent conversation was not only tolerated by Tang Xuanzong but amused the emperor so much that he gave the poet a post in the imperial academy—despite the fact that Li Bai had passed none of the official examinations normally required for such a position. Doubtless Li Bai's success was in part due to his own account of himself, which has come down to us in his letters. He claimed kinship with the imperial family because they shared the same family name, and presented himself as an aristocrat who had spent his fortune helping others. These and other such statements are considered by some scholars to be the highly questionable assertions of an ambitious young man of obscure origin bent on achieving recognition; many of the recorded incidents of his life, such as the following, may be presumed to be apocryphal.

Li Bai, a talented linguist as well as a poet, was summoned to court one day to translate a document that had come from a vassal state. He arrived so drunk that the first thing he did was to vomit all over the emperor's clothes. Then, while the emperor cleaned up the mess with his own handkerchief, Li Bai ordered the lady Yang Guifei to prepare the writing materials for him and grind up some ink. Only when all was arranged for his convenience did Li Bai write out the translation.

It is not surprising that Li Bai wore out his welcome at court, especially so far as Yang Guifei was concerned; in fact, she ultimately persuaded the emperor not to receive the Banished Immortal again. After less than three years in Chang'an, the poet left and wandered through the empire, hoping for, but never finding, patronage elsewhere. He also spent much time in the provinces

Figure 31. This album-leaf painting by the Qing dynasty artist Yuan Yao, and titled "Chenxiang Pavilion," shows the poet Li Bai (on the lower right, supported by a courtier) as he approaches the pavilion inside which the Tang emperor Xuanzong and the lady Yang Guifei await his inspired presence. Phoenix Art Museum, museum purchase with funds provided, in part, by an anonymous donor

near Hangzhou and is buried in the village of Dangtu in Anhui province. During his lifetime, he was not widely known. Only after the poets of the ninth century acclaimed his genius was his fame assured. It rests on his ability to infuse the tradition-ladened forms of Chinese poetry with a unique personal quality. The following poem treats an ancient theme, and one that is hardly peculiar to China:

> *Endless yearning*
> *Here in Ch'ang-an*
> *Where the cricket spinners cry autumn*
> *by the rail of the golden well,*
> *Where flecks of frost blow chill,*
> *and the bedmat's color, cold.*

No light from the lonely lantern,
the longing almost broken—
Then roll up the curtain, gaze on the moon,
heave the sigh that does no good.
A lady lovely like the flowers,
beyond that wall of clouds,
And above, the blue dark of heavens high,
And below, the waves of pale waters.
Endless the sky, far the journey,
the fleet soul suffers in flight,
And in its dreams can't touch its goal
through the fastness of barrier mountains—
Then endless yearning
Crushes a man's heart.[2]

The legend of Li Bai's death is in keeping with those of his life. While drunk one moonlit night, he went out fishing. As he leaned over the side of the boat and tried to embrace the moon's watery reflection, he fell into the river and drowned. Perhaps he was reaching for a scene from another of his poems:

At Autumn Cove, so many white monkeys
bounding, leaping up like snowflakes in flight!
They coax and pull their young ones down from branches
to drink and frolic with the water-borne moon.[3]

---

2. Li Bai, in Stephen Owen, *The Great Age of Chinese Poetry: The High Tang* (New Haven: Yale University Press, 1981), 127.
3. Li Bai, in Burton Watson, *The Columbia Book of Chinese Poetry* (New York: Columbia University Press, 1984), 209.

8

THE THIRD PERIOD OF
DISUNITY AND THE
SONG DYNASTY

907–1279

The partitioning of China that occurred at the end of the Tang dynasty lasted for fifty-three years, a period generally called the Five Dynasties. In North China, these five decades were a time of unrelieved fighting as five dynasties replaced one another in quick succession: the Later Liang, the Later Tang, the Later Jin, the Later Han, and the Later Zhou. However, in South China, it was an era of relative peace and prosperity as smaller divisions, known as the Ten Kingdoms, stayed more or less in place. These leave us with another list of confusing names: Wu, Wuyue, Southern Han, Chu, Former Shu, Min, Jingnan, Later Shu, Southern Tang, and Northern Han. Meanwhile, north of the Great Wall, a new phenomenon was the arrival of the Qidan [Ch'i-tan] (also Khitan), a Mongolian tribe who conquered all the other tribes living north of the Great Wall, from Inner Mongolia to the Sea of Japan. By 916, the Qidan had established their own dynastic rule. The new name they chose reflected their warlike nature: Liao, or "Iron." Then, in 960, while the Liao stayed in place, everything south of the Great Wall came back together under a new Chinese dynasty, the Song [Sung].

This arrangement was more or less stable until 1127, when the Liao, who by now held some of the territory south of the Great

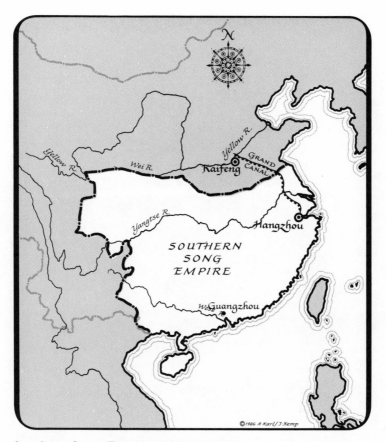

Southern Song Empire (1127–1279)

Wall, were overthrown in turn by the Nüzhen [Nuchen] (also called Juchen and Jürchen), a Tatar tribe from northern Manchuria who had been vassals to the Liao. The Nüzhen pushed even further south to occupy the northern half of the Song empire and established *their* dynastic rule, contrasting themselves with the Liao by taking the name Jin [Chin], or "Gold." The Jin ruled until 1234. (Despite the similar romanization, the character for this Tatar Jin dynasty is different in form and meaning from the previous Western, Eastern, and Later Jin dynasties established by the Chinese.)

The Song dynasty, now known as the Southern Song, continued to rule over South China until 1279.

Keeping this chronology in mind, let us backtrack to the start of the Song unification of the empire in 960.

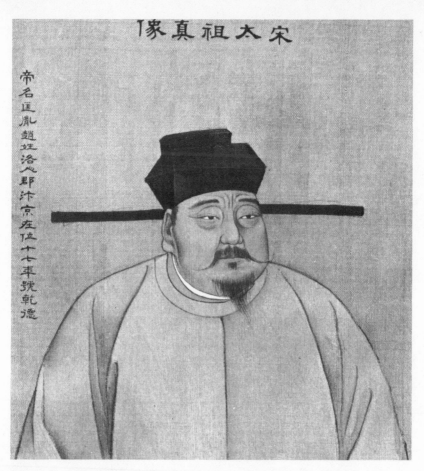

Figure 32. Song Taizu persuaded his generals to retire to a life of civilian comfort, and put civil officials in charge of a centrally managed army. The Metropolitan Museum of Art, gift of Mrs. Edward S. Harkness, 1947

Song Taizu [Sung Tai-tsu]

Song Taizu (r. 960–976), which means Song Grand Ancestor, is nicknamed the Reluctant Emperor. As the commander of the Imperial Guard of the Later Zhou (one of the Five Dynasties), he led a successful expedition along the northern border against the Liao. His officers decided that he would make a better emperor than the ineffectual young man who sat on the Later Zhou throne. They came to their general in his tent, woke him from sleep, and insisted, with drawn swords, that he lead them back to take the Later Zhou capital and put himself on the throne. The general, after going through the motions of protesting his loyalty to the boy emperor, carried out his coup d'état. He founded the Song dynasty in 960 and led his army to conquer the southern Ten Kingdoms. He chose Kaifeng as his capital and decreed that the color of the imperial robes be brown.

Soon after, when his authority was challenged by the rebellion of some of the very men who had insisted that he be emperor, Song Taizu invited his officers to a great banquet and said to them:

"It is not easy to be the emperor. Every night I toss in my bed as I consider the power you have to overthrow me. You profess loyalty just as I once did to the emperor of the Later Zhou, but one day you may be persuaded to turn against me.

"Now, life is too short to be spent in endless battles, and most of us desire instead peace and prosperity and heirs for our fortunes. I propose to you all that you resign your military commissions, in return for which I will give you posts in the empire where you can prosper, make money, buy lands for yourselves and your heirs, and live happy and long lives."

These words touched the hearts of his audience, and one by one they relinquished their military commands to him and retired to civilian life.

In the same vein, under a successor of Song Taizu, a great scholar-statesman proposed sweeping reforms for the sake of continued peace and prosperity in the empire. This was Wang Anshi, who, as the contemporary of William the Conqueror, is a useful figure in marking the comparative developments of Chinese and European civilization.

Wang Anshi [Wang An-shih]

Wang Anshi (1021–1086) is considered the second great reformer in Chinese history. The first was Wang Mang, whose reforms at the beginning of the first century A.D., when he had usurped the Han throne, led to his decapitation. Wang Anshi did not aspire to the throne, nor did he come to quite such a violent end. He was a scholar of wide-ranging knowledge and interests who became

Figure 33. Wang Anshi, as prime minister to a Northern Song emperor, tried to implement social and economic reforms.

prime minister to the sixth Northern Song emperor. He was familiar with medicine and plant life, with agriculture and even weaving, but primarily he was a social philosopher who saw the need for legislation, New Laws as he called them, to ensure the proper use of government funds, the paring down of the bureaucracy, the equitable distribution of grain, and fair pricing for peasants selling farm produce. These economic reforms were inimical to the interests of the top-heavy administration. His plan for social reform, which included the creation of ten-family units in which wrongdoers were to be monitored by other members within the unit, was resisted in his day but presaged the work cadres and family units of mid-twentieth-century China. Wang Anshi, a man ahead of his time, died in disheartened retirement.

Song Huizong [Sung Hui-tsung]

Fourteen years after Wang Anshi's death, Song Huizong (r. 1100–1125), eighth Northern Song emperor, took the throne. He is the most touchingly tragic figure in Chinese history. His great passion was collecting "old masters" and he instructed his agents to confiscate for his specially built museum any great works of art found

Figure 34. The artist-emperor Song Huizong lost half the empire and died a prisoner in the wilds of Manchuria. The Metropolitan Museum of Art, gift of Mrs. Edward S. Harkness, 1947

in the homes of his subjects. He was himself an accomplished artist and, while he made copies of former works, he also originated a new literal style of painting birds and animals, or "feather and fur," as the Chinese call this genre. He invited artists to join in competitions in his palace/academy of art where he proposed themes and gave prizes for the most faithful renditions of nature. Some of his originals are now treasured in museum collections, and usually include samples of yet another of his accomplishments—his own "lean gold style" of calligraphy.

85

Figure 35. The emperor Song Huizong is renowned for his paintings of birds and flowers. The above detail from his hand scroll Five-Colored Parakeet *is accompanied (opposite) by his characteristic calligraphy.* Courtesy of the Museum of Fine Arts, Boston, Maria Antoinette Evans Fund

Song Huizong's devotion to art was matched by his devotion to philosophical and religious matters. During the eleventh century, Confucianism, Daoism, and Buddhism had all been the subjects of renewed study and interpretation. It was during this time that Daoism as a religion acquired a pantheon of deities, and Huizong, in his day, became fascinated with a Daoist deity. According to some accounts, he even identified himself with this personage and fancied that he saw his heavenly palace floating in the sky and longed for the day when he could return to it.

This was the wrong moment for a dreamer to be seated on the throne. As we have seen, by this time the Liao had conquered an area traditionally a part of China's empires—the area around present-day Beijing, south of the Great Wall. Huizong, when he turned his attention to affairs-of-state, imagined bringing this territory back within the imperial boundary but recognized that he

86

五色鸚鵡來自嶺表養之禁
籞馴服可愛飛鳴自適往來
於苑囿間方中春繁杏遍開
翔翥其上雅詫容與自有一
種態度縱目觀之宛勝圖畫
因賦是詩焉
天產乾皋此異禽遐陬來貢九重深
體全五色非凡質惠吐多言更好音
飛翥似憐毛羽貴徘徊如飽稻粱心
緗膺紺趾誠端雅為賦新篇步武吟

needed help. He turned to the Nüzhen, mentioned at the start of the chapter, a tribe eager to challenge the Liao, and whose people, at the start of the twelfth century, still lived a nomad-hunter life in the plains and forests of northern Manchuria. Their leader was a man whose instinct for tribal organization was equal to his effectiveness as a warrior on horseback. The artistic Huizong could not have chosen a more unsuitable ally, but blinded by his vision of a reunified empire south of the Great Wall, he naïvely proposed a deal to this rough-and-ready "barbarian." Once the Liao were defeated, he said, the Nüzhen could have all the lands north of the Great Wall while he would keep the lands to the south.

This proposal proved suicidal. The Nüzhen swept down and took over the Liao lands, including the Beijing area south of the Great Wall, but not only did they not hand the latter over to Huizong, they pushed on to blockade the capital of Kaifeng. Huizong was captured and taken to live out the last nine years of his life as a beggar at the mercy of crude Nüzhen tribesmen in the northern forests—far from his palace full of beautiful paintings and philosophical texts. One can only hope that he found solace in renewed visions of heavenly palaces, for he certainly had no earthly pleasures to enjoy.

Meanwhile, in 1127, the Song court fled south from the besieged capital to a new one at Lin'an, or Temporary Peace (now the city of Hangzhou). From here Southern Song (as opposed to Northern Song) rule was established over what was left of the empire; it lasted until 1279. During this century and a half, a constant debate raged within the imperial court between those who advocated fighting for the reconquest of North China and those who favored relinquishing even more territories to the nomadic invaders. The emperors and the upper class of scholar-officials, both at court and in the provinces, were all in the latter camp. This small, affluent segment of society preferred indulging in a life of luxury to waging war. In the capital every kind of specialty shop existed. Merchants, no longer supplied by caravans crossing Central Asia, depended on sea trade for exotic produce from the island kingdoms of the South China Sea and India.

The Southern Song emperors and their empresses set ever higher artistic and intellectual standards as they continued Song Huizong's aesthetic pursuits, devoting themselves to painting, the study of philosophy, and the collecting and printing of books on all subjects. They especially favored small, intimate scenes featuring flora and fauna on fans, album leaves, and scrolls. In the hands of Song potters, porcelain, a hard, translucent ceramic ware invented during the Tang dynasty, was shaped into simple, elegant forms covered in subtle tones of jade, ivory, and beige.

In the thirteenth century, the refined civilization of the Song world was suddenly shattered, like one of its porcelains swept from a shelf, by the invasion of the great Mongolian horde led by Genghis Khan. For over three thousand years the Chinese had fought off barbarian invasions, and even when they lost North China, they had maintained a sovereign state in South China. This time the barbarians were indomitable, and the Middle Kingdom became a mere piece of the vast Mongolian empire.

A poignant event marks the end of both the Song era and the much longer stretch of unbroken Chinese self-rule. In 1280, pursued by the Mongols, the child heir to the Song throne was brought

Figure 36. Song potters, like the anonymous craftsman who fashioned this vase, achieved new heights of stylistic and technical refinement. Courtesy of the Freer Gallery of Art, Smithsonian Institution, Washington, D.C.

by his loyal minister to the harbor near Guangzhou, where they boarded a boat. The Mongol armies caught up with them and cornered them on board this vessel, whereupon the minister took the boy on his back, and together they jumped into the sea and drowned.

9

THE FIRST FOREIGN RULE: THE YUAN DYNASTY

1271–1368

The next dynastic phase of Chinese history must be prefaced with a brief description of the great Mongolian leader Genghis Khan, or Chinggis Khan, founder of the largest empire the world has ever known. (Although the Mongolian conquests were vaster than those of Attila the Hun, eight hundred years earlier, they did not reach Western Europe. There, while Genghis and his heirs devastated kingdoms and empires from Korea to Hungary, King Richard the Lion-Hearted led a crusade to the Middle East, Robin Hood reigned in Sherwood Forest, Saint Francis of Assisi founded a monastic order, and during the reign of Louis IX, the great cathedral at Chartres rose from the French plains.)

Genghis Khan was born in the middle of the twelfth century to a Mongolian chieftain. While still a boy, known then as Temuchin, his father died, and he and his brothers were ostracized from their father's tribe and left to fend for themselves, scrounging for roots, berries, and game and developing ruthless combative skills as they defended themselves against inhospitable members of their tribe.

Temuchin excelled at setting his enemies at one another's throats and then moving in for the kill. He was a born leader and, as a young man, gained a following that grew until he became the ruler

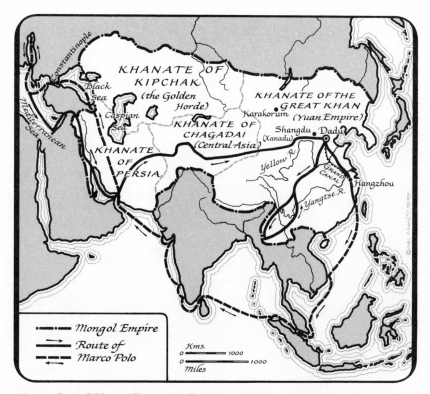

Mongol and Yuan Dynasty Empires (1271–1368)

of all the Mongolian tribes and took the name Genghis Khan, "Universal Ruler." He conquered lands to the west as far as southern Russia; to the south, he made significant inroads into the Jin empire.

At his death in 1227, he left four great kingdoms to four of his descendants—southern Russia, Persia, Central Asia, and Mongolia/North China. Ogdai, ruler of the latter, was declared the Great Khan and made his capital at Karakorum, in Mongolia. He was informed about the continuing campaigns of conquest in Russia through an unprecedented post system: His couriers, supplied with fresh horses at well-manned stations, were able to travel two hundred miles a day. News of Ogdai's death in 1241 traveled from Karakorum to Hungary in a matter of days.

It was Ogdai's third successor, his nephew Kublai Khan, who conquered South China. He not only incorporated it into the Mongol Empire but established a new dynastic era in China itself.

Figure 37. Genghis Khan's grandson, Kublai Khan, was the first "barbarian" to conquer all of China. The Metropolitan Museum of Art, gift of Mrs. Edward S. Harkness, 1947

Kublai Khan

Kublai Khan, also spelled Khubilai Khan or Kubla Khan (1215?–1294), was a grandson of Genghis Khan and founded the Yuan (meaning "first" or "original") dynasty that ruled over China from 1271 to 1368 (some chronologies date it 1279–1368) with eleven Mongol emperors. He chose a new capital city, called Khanbuluc by the Mongols and Dadu [Tatu] by the Chinese, located in what is now the northern section of Beijing.

Earlier in his career, Kublai had fought under his uncle, Ogdai, helping him to conquer the Southern Song territories. He was named the fifth Great Khan of the Mongols in 1260, but it was not until 1271 that he declared himself emperor of China as well. Even so, the Song fought on to the bitter end, holding their capital until 1276; most histories date the official end of the Song in 1279.

Kublai Khan was fascinated by the Chinese culture, and although he had been uncompromising in the battle for supremacy, he now turned to providing stability for his new subjects and to the assimilation of their culture. He realized that the first order of business for a ruler in China was water control and canal building. The Yellow River was given a new course, and another Grand Canal was built linking the new capital with the rice-producing south.

Kublai Khan encouraged Chinese painters to live at court, practiced ancestor worship, followed Buddhist teachings, and tried to gain the allegiance of the scholars. But all this did not win the hearts of the Chinese people, who regarded Kublai Khan and all other Yuan emperors as foreigners. The following story speaks volumes.

A Song general who had been captured when the Mongolians took control was imprisoned in the capital. Kublai Khan realized that winning the loyalty of this man would help to diminish Chinese resentment of his rule, so he offered the general his freedom in exchange for his loyal service as a high official. The general replied:

"My one wish is to be put to death. Without the Song dynasty to serve, my life has no purpose."

The general's wish was granted, and Kublai Khan chose a non-Chinese to fill the post.

With Central Asia under Mongolian control, traders were once again able to pass from West to East and back. It is thanks to one of these men, Marco Polo, that faraway Europe became aware of China and her amazing culture. Although this man's accounts are regarded by many as highly exaggerated, and the manuscripts upon which the modern version of his story is based conflict in many details, the consensus is that he has left us a lively and basically reliable picture of Kublai Khan, his palaces, and the China he ruled.

Figure 38. Marco Polo (the horseman in the middle), shown leaving Venice with his father and uncle, became an ambassador at the court of Kublai Khan. Bibliothèque Nationale, Paris

Marco Polo

Marco Polo (1254–1324) was the son of a Venetian merchant. He was not the first European to visit China. His father and uncle had traveled to the court of Kublai Khan and had returned to Venice with an invitation to come back to China with a hundred Christian priests, letters from the Pope, and holy water from Jerusalem. Before Kublai's rule, Louis IX of France had sent priests to the court of Mangu Khan in 1253. (Mangu Khan was Ogdai's second successor and Kublai Khan's older brother.) Mangu considered them envoys from a vassal kingdom and sent the priests home with a message asking that the French pay tribute to China. In contrast, Kublai Khan was curious about Christianity and expected that a hundred priests would tell him all there was to know about it.

In 1271 the Polo brothers and Marco, then seventeen, started out with only two priests, some holy water, and a papal document; the two priests turned homeward at the first opportunity, leaving the three Polos to proceed to the court of Kublai Khan. Even without clerical support, they were warmly received there. Marco became a favorite with the Great Khan and served him as a roving ambassador for twenty years. He returned to Venice in 1294, promptly took the losing side of a political battle, and landed in prison. His bad luck was our good fortune. Marco spent his days in prison telling tales of his fabulous travels in the Orient, and his cellmate, a literate minstrel, recorded it all. Marco's vivid account has survived in a variety of languages and editions and was the source for the nineteenth-century English poet Coleridge's famous lines "In Xanadu did Kubla Khan/A stately pleasure-dome decree. . . ." Marco's tales provide a wonderful if not wholly accurate account of life in thirteenth-century China. Here are three samplings:

On Shangdu (Coleridge's Xanadu):

[The traveler] comes to a city called Shang-tu, which was built by the Great Khan now reigning. . . . In this city Kublai Khan built a huge palace of marble and other ornamental stones. Its halls and chambers are all gilded, and the whole building is marvellously embellished and richly adorned. At one end it extends into the middle of the city, at the other it abuts on the city wall. At this end, another wall, running out from the city wall in the direction opposite to the palace, encloses and encircles fully sixteen miles of parkland well watered with springs and streams and diversified with lawns. Into this park there is no entry except by way of the palace. Here the great Khan keeps game animals of all sorts. . . . the gerfalcons alone amount to more than 200 . . . often he enters the park with a leopard on the crupper of his horse; when he feels inclined, he lets it go and thus catches a hart or stag or roebuck to give to the gerfalcons that he keeps in the mew. And this he does for recreation and sport.[1]

1. Ronald Latham, trans., *Marco Polo, the Travels* (New York: Penguin Books, 1982), 108.

On the old Southern Song capital city of Hangzhou:

> The city . . . is about 100 miles in circumference, because its streets and watercourses are wide and spacious. Then there are market-places, which because of the multitudes that throng them must be very large and spacious. The layout of the city is as follows. On one side is a lake of fresh water, very clear. On the other is a huge river, which entering by many channels, diffused throughout the city, carries away all its filth and then flows into the lake, from which it flows out towards the Ocean. This makes the air very wholesome. . . . There are said to be 12,000 bridges, mostly of stone, though some are of wood. Those over the main channels and the chief thoroughfare are built with such lofty arches and so well designed that big ships can pass under them without a mast, and yet over them pass carts and horses; so well are the street-levels adjusted to the height. . . . Among the articles regularly on sale [in the market] squares are all sorts of vegetables and fruits, above all huge pears, weighing 10 lb. apiece, white as dough inside and very fragrant . . . every day a vast quantity of fish is brought upstream from the ocean. . . . Other streets are occupied by women of the town . . . attired with great magnificence, heavily perfumed, attended by many handmaids and lodged in richly ornamented apartments. These ladies are highly proficient and accomplished in the uses of endearments and caresses, with words suited and adapted to every sort of person, so that foreigners who have once enjoyed them remain utterly beside themselves and so captivated by their sweetness and charm that they can never forget them.[2]

He recorded the resentment the subjected Chinese felt toward both the Mongolian ruler and the other foreigners he assigned to government posts:

2. Ibid., 216 ff. This description of Hangzhou continues for almost twenty pages.

You must understand that all the Cathayans hated the government of the Great Khan, because he set over them Tartar rulers, mostly Saracens, and they could not endure it, since it made them feel that they were no more than slaves. Moreover, the Great Khan had no legal title to rule the province of Cathay, having acquired it by force.[3]

After less than a hundred years, the Yuan emperors who succeeded Kublai Khan began to trade the warrior life of their ancestors for a life of luxury behind palace walls, until finally they became powerless against the growing unrest of the Chinese people. Eventually the uprisings of secret societies, most notably that of the Red Scarves (also known as the Red Turbans), led by Zhu Yuanzhang [Chu Yuan-chang], succeeded in overthrowing the Yuan dynasty and restoring Chinese rule under the Ming dynasty.

3. Ibid., 133. The term *Cathay* refers to North China.

10

THE MING DYNASTY
AND THE COMING OF
THE WESTERNERS
1368–1644

The Ming dynasty, founded immediately on the heels of the Yuan, ruled from 1368 to 1644 under sixteen emperors. These Ming emperors were the last truly Chinese dynasts. Their capital was established first at Nanjing (Nanking), or "Southern Capital," and then at Beijing ("Northern Capital"). The monuments of Ming architecture still standing in and near Beijing—the Forbidden City, the Temple to Heaven, the great underground Ming tombs, the rebuilt Great Wall—symbolize the consolidation of Ming power.

Ming Taizu [Ming Tai-tsu]

Ming ("Bright") Taizu ("Grand Ancestor") is the posthumous title of the founder and first emperor of the Ming dynasty, who ruled from 1368 to 1398. Ming Taizu, sometimes nicknamed the Beggar King, came from a poor family and, as a youth, had been a Buddhist monk. His original name was Zhu Yuanzhang, and as such he joined the Red Scarves in their rebellion against Yuan rule; he led the capture of Nanjing in 1356 and, twelve years later, chased the last Yuan emperor from Beijing. After declaring the new "Bright"

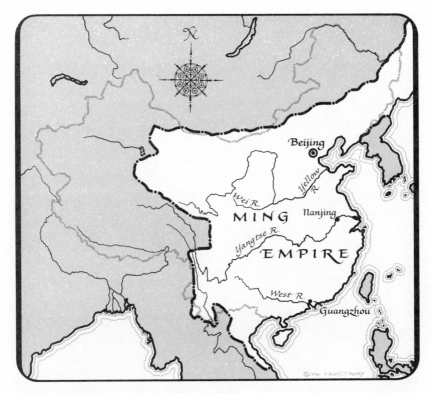

Ming Dynasty Empire (1368–1644)

dynasty, he pursued the Mongol forces far north of the Great Wall and, for the first time in Chinese history, took the lands of Manchuria along the Sea of Japan.

Ming Taizu devoted his reign to restoring Chinese political and cultural autonomy. He reestablished schools, libraries, and the examination system for the selection of civil servants—all of which had been neglected under Mongolian rule. Despite his fondness for Buddhism, he, like Tang Taizong, declared Confucianism the state doctrine. However, he did not rule in the manner of the Confucian sages. Instead, he turned on those who had helped him seize the throne and, in the course of his reign, ordered the execution of three prime ministers, whom he accused of treachery, and thousands of their supposed supporters. He finally abolished the office of prime minister and replaced it with that of grand secretary. The office of prime minister dated back to the early Shang dynasty. Traditionally, according to Confucian doctrine, the

Figure 39. Ming Taizu reclaimed the empire from the Mongols. His extraordinary jutting chin makes him easily recognizable. The Metropolitan Museum of Art, gift of Mrs. Edward S. Harkness, 1947

appointees to this post should be men of wisdom and high moral character who guided and tempered autocratic power in the interests of the general welfare while they performed the duties of chief administrator of the government. By the fourteenth century, a man had to prove himself worthy of this role through scholarly achievement. In contrast, Ming Taizu's appointee as grand secretary, although he was a scholar-official, did not offer advice but merely recorded the emperor's edicts in elegant phrases and calligraphy. The emperor took over the role of the prime minister and became chief executive over his civil servants. All subsequent

明成祖真像

帝名棣太祖四子在位二十二年號永樂

Figure 40. The Yongle emperor usurped the throne, made Beijing his capital, and set a new imperial style in dragon robes, like the one he wears here. The Metropolitan Museum of Art, gift of Mrs. Edward S. Harkness, 1947

Ming emperors copied this administrative model, but with the exception of the Yongle emperor, they were unable to fill their role adequately and became increasingly the puppets of both their grand secretaries and the chief eunuchs.

Ming Taizu, shortly before his death at seventy-one, chose his young grandson, son of his deceased eldest son, as heir. He purposely passed over his other sons because he considered them ambitious to the point of disloyalty. This judgment was justified posthumously when the unfortunate grandson was displaced by one of his uncles, best known as the Yongle emperor.

101

The Yongle [Yung Lo] Emperor

The title Yongle ("Perpetual Happiness") is not the name of the emperor but the name of a reign, so we refer to the Yongle emperor or the emperor of the Yongle reign. Though he is most commonly referred to this way, this emperor also had a posthumous dynastic title, Chengzu [Ch'eng-tsu] ("Successful Progenitor"), and a forbidden family name, Zhudi [Chu-ti]. (See chapter 5 for an explanation of imperial nomenclature.)

The Yongle emperor (r. 1402–24), fourth son of Ming Taizu, succeeded, after a four-year struggle, in taking the throne from his teenage nephew. The deposed young man escaped, disguised as a Buddhist monk; he never recaptured his throne, and only years later was it known that he had lived out his life hidden in a series of remote monasteries.

In order to strengthen the newly acquired northern section of the empire, the Yongle emperor moved the capital from Nanjing to Beijing. The new Ming capital, completed in 1421, was built in part over the southern area of the old Yuan capital. It consisted of three walled rectangles, one inside the other, erected along a north-south axis. These were the Inner City, the Imperial City, where court officials lived, and the Forbidden City, or Imperial Palace. Directly south of and adjacent to the inner city was the walled-in outer city, whose principal features were the ceremonial altars to heaven and agriculture. Each of these cities was defined by massive walls, although today only those around the Forbidden City remain; the outer series of walls was destroyed during the Cultural Revolution in the 1970s. The Forbidden City is now called the Palace Museum and is open to visitors. (During the Qing dynasty, when the Manchu conquerors inhabited all three walled-in areas, the Chinese were allowed to live in the area directly to the south, which then became known as the Chinese city.)

The Forbidden City, off limits to the common subject, embodied the total separation between ruler and ruled. There is no palace in the Western hemisphere which has quite the massive presence of this complex. The scale of its 250 acres makes the human figure shrink to insectlike proportions. Thirty-five-feet-high walls define a rectangle a thousand yards from north to south and eight hundred

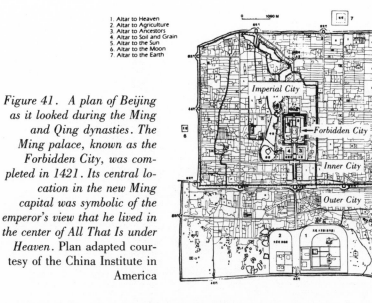

1. Altar to Heaven
2. Altar to Agriculture
3. Altar to Ancestors
4. Altar to Soil and Grain
5. Altar to the Sun
6. Altar to the Moon
7. Altar to the Earth

Figure 41. A plan of Beijing as it looked during the Ming and Qing dynasties. The Ming palace, known as the Forbidden City, was completed in 1421. Its central location in the new Ming capital was symbolic of the emperor's view that he lived in the center of All That Is under Heaven. Plan adapted courtesy of the China Institute in America

Figure 42. This turn-of-the-century view south, from Coal Hill, shows the rooftops of the Forbidden City. Library of Congress

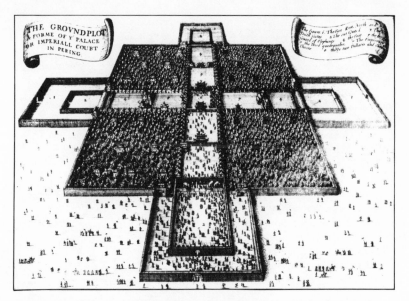

Figure 43. This seventeenth-century English etching of the Forbidden City completely misrepresents its plan and scale. The result resembles a large walled English garden.

Figure 44. Court officials stand in ranked attendance on the emperor, who sits in the center distance on the throne in the audience hall. This 1830s European illustration, which shows the scale of the palace more accurately than Figure 43, must be based on firsthand knowledge of the Forbidden City. New York Public Library Picture Collection

yards from east to west. (Outside these walls, no one was allowed to build any structure taller than the imperial buildings.) Each wall contains one gate, but the official gate, called Wumen ("Meridian Gate"), is centered in the south wall. Inside, moving north, one crosses a vast courtyard to another wall and gate. Beyond a second courtyard, this one large enough to hold ninety thousand officials and divided by an artificial river crossed by five bridges, rises the 115-foot-high Hall of Supreme Harmony. Here, and in the two slightly smaller halls to the north, each preceded by its own courtyard, the emperors held audiences and officiated at ceremonies. When not so occupied, they retreated into the imperial living quarters and gardens which occupy the northernmost half of the Forbidden City. The Ming emperors lived lives all but unseen; in some cases they did not set foot outside the Forbidden City for decades. They lived within walls within walls within walls, and the commoner outside knew only that inside was contained the power which inflexibly controlled his life.

That the scale of this palace was inconceivable to the European imagination is apparent when one looks at Western engravings of the Forbidden City, which make the buildings look cute and too small in relation to human figures.

The Yongle emperor, the only effective emperor to succeed the dynastic founder, consolidated Chinese culture through the enormous project of collecting over seven thousand texts, which were reproduced and cataloged in his famous *Yongle Encyclopedia*. This massive work kept many scholars fully employed for a lifetime. It also saved many of these texts from oblivion, and we are indebted to the Yongle emperor for perceiving the necessity of this archival task. Since the Chinese characters cannot be arranged alphabetically, the materials are organized by phonetic rhymes.

Zheng He [Cheng Ho]

The greatest, and really the only, navigational expeditions in Chinese history took place during the Yongle reign. These expeditions were led by Zheng He, a Muslim eunuch who became an admiral in the Yongle court.

One explanation given in traditional Chinese histories for this

Figure 45. This seagoing junk is the descendant of the even bigger crafts that the Ming admiral Zheng He sailed as far as East Africa in the early fifteenth century. Library of Congress

sudden and unique spurt of seabound exploration is that the Yongle emperor wanted to find his deposed nephew, who was said to have fled by boat to a Buddhist monastery on some island in the South Seas. Recent scholarship amends this theory by suggesting that these expeditions were inspired by the emperor's eagerness to let the world know of his supreme sovereignty and his interest in receiving valuable tributes from any would-be colonies. Zheng He's fleet consisted of sixty-three oceangoing junks, the largest of which were 440 feet long and 180 feet wide and carried over four hundred men each—easily the largest ships of their day. They sailed first to what is now Indonesia, where the admiral found not the emperor's nephew but a native king, whom he brought back to the

106

Forbidden City to pay homage to the Yongle emperor. Zheng He made seven other long expeditions and got as far as the east coast of Africa. He brought back no further kings but did return with an immense amount of geographic information as well as animals never before seen in China: ostriches, zebras, and giraffes.

Nothing that Zheng He brought back to court dissuaded the Yongle emperor from the traditional notion that the Chinese emperor was the ruler of "all that is under Heaven," including any lands reached by Zheng He. The only voice of dissent came from the Japanese, whose pirates operated in the Sea of Japan and along the coasts of the newly acquired Ming territories in Manchuria. When the emperor sent orders that they stop their ravages, they dared to reply that heaven and earth were not the monopoly of one ruler and that the world belonged to itself, not to any individual!

Zheng He's expeditions continued after the death of the Yongle emperor, till 1433. After that, the Chinese made no further attempts to explore, conquer, or even reconnoiter by sea. Since Zheng He's personal account of his expeditions was destroyed by rivals within the Ming court, we can suppose that the scholar-administrators close to the emperors disapproved of costly naval voyages to lands across the seas, giving priority to the traditional concerns of protecting the northern and western borders. Whether this was the case or not, China lost her one opportunity to beat the West to the colonization of the islands of the South Seas, and her inward focus made it impossible for her to hold her own as the West moved into the Chinese sphere of influence.

The older it got, the more rigid the Ming dynasty became. Even the actual human being who was emperor was merely a pawn in the system. The fascinating portrait of the Ming world presented by Ray Huang in *1587, A Year of No Significance* makes it clear that it was not possible for rulers to govern according to a moral code, as prescribed in Confucian teachings, when confronted by the corruption, disloyalty, and abuse of power endemic in the Ming world.

The cultural focus of the Ming era was on the past. This was true in both art and literature. Ming painters looked over their shoulders to the past art of the Tang and the Song and tried to recapture the spirit of landscapes and flora and fauna as rendered in past centuries. Although there was a wide variety of techniques and approaches, these were applied to traditional themes.

In ceramics, Ming artisans further refined the porcelain techniques of the Song with new decorative patterns and glazes that gave dazzling surfaces to elegant dishes. It was during the Ming dynasty that the blue and white patterns so popular in the West and copied on the Dutch delftware were first produced.

And so we arrive at the time when the Chinese and the Europeans came into constant contact with each other. Before this there had been only indirect trade through the middlemen of Central Asia and India, but now, in the sixteenth century, Europeans discovered navigational routes to the fabulous land of China.

Western Mercantile and Missionary Contacts

Less than a hundred years after Zheng He's last naval expedition, the first Portuguese ships arrived at the Chinese coast near Guangzhou in 1514. The Chinese now met a new kind of "barbarian": strange creatures with wide, round eyes and noses which were long and beaklike. "Foreign devils" was the Chinese epithet for these visitors from the West.

In 1516 eight Portuguese ships sailed upriver to Guangzhou and sent an envoy with a letter from the king of Portugal to the emperor. While the fleet waited for the emperor's reply, the captain's brother built a fort, robbed Chinese vessels, kidnapped women and children, and in general behaved with total disrespect for the Chinese. As a result, the envoy to the emperor was considered a spy and was sent back to Guangzhou and thrown in prison along with several others of the Portuguese party. The rest were sent away.

This episode characterizes the Chinese experience with European contacts from this time on. The Chinese did not seek foreign contact. It was the Europeans who sought trade and commerce with them. Furthermore, it was the European view that the interests of these Eastern peoples with their exotic customs could simply be disregarded; they were there for the Westerner to exploit. If one bears this in mind, it is not strange that the Chinese were at times violently hostile to the Western presence.

Since the fourteenth century, Marco Polo's account of Cathay (a name for China used in Europe and derived from Polo's reference to Qidan [Mongol] people) had been amplified by Arab traders who brought spices and silks from the East. In 1492 Columbus was seeking a new route to this fabled land when he came instead upon the Caribbean islands. The discovery of the so-called New World did not stop the search. The Portuguese found the route to Cathay around the Cape of Good Hope, arriving, as noted above, in 1514. But it was not until the middle of the seventeenth century that the English followed their lead and landed downriver from Guangzhou. Forewarned by the Portuguese experience, they fired their cannons as they made their way upriver to the city, where they traded their cargo. This was an unpleasant way to do business.

Missionaries followed fast in the wake of the first Western traders. The best known of these is Matteo Ricci (1552–1610). He was a Jesuit from Italy who arrived in Macao in 1582. He learned Chinese, took a Chinese name, Li Madou [Li Ma-tou], and wore the robes of a Confucian scholar, which impressed the Chinese with the notion that Christianity and Confucianism had something in common. After twenty years, he was allowed to travel to Beijing, where he presented the emperor with a harpsichord, two chiming clocks, and a map of the world. He became a science tutor to the emperor's son, and his effectiveness in preaching the Gospel was considerable, for at his death in 1610, there were over three hundred Catholic churches in the Ming empire.

The Jesuit presence at the Chinese court involved a lifetime commitment on the part of these priests; the Chinese would not let them return to Europe. Their lives at court brought more than a new theology to the Chinese, for the Jesuits were highly trained in mathematics and the sciences. Even though the Catholic Church was conservative in such matters, these priests made their Chinese students aware of a new scientific attitude.

Chinese technology had preceded that of the West in many areas: The first eclipses were recorded in China; the first iron was cast in China; and silk, paper, and gunpowder were invented in China centuries before they were introduced to the West. All sorts of mechanical devices, such as compasses, clocks, wheelbarrows, and water pumps, were originally invented by the Chinese. But, as Joseph Needham, the great documenter of Chinese science, points out, the Chinese genius was based on what he calls "organic materialism," which sought to make all phenomena fit into a closed, hierarchical organization. The understanding of how the pieces fit together was based on the interpretations of the *I-ching*, the book of diagrams used for millennia by the Chinese in interpreting natural phenomena (see chapter 3 under Confucius). What the Jesuits brought, despite their own church's resistance to figures like Galileo, was the science that began with him, a science based on the experimental verification of hypotheses and the continual revision of such findings in accordance with accumulating data. In this method—which we call "modern" science—phenomena, as revealed through experimentation, force man constantly to amend his view of the universal order. As Needham points out, this approach differs from previous scientific attitudes in that it does not depend on, and can exist independently of, the cultural environment. In direct contrast with, for instance, traditional Chinese science, or the science of medieval Europe, the purpose of which is to confirm a philosophical or religious point of view, whether of the *I-ching* or the Catholic Church, modern science is culturally neutral.

The Jesuits were useful to the Chinese, but only up to a point. As we shall see, during the centuries to follow, their presence, and that of other Christian missionaries, would become highly controversial.

11

THE QING DYNASTY AND THE CONTINUED WESTERN PRESENCE

1644–1911

T he Ming rule ground on in place for two hundred years before uprisings in the south and invasion from the north combined to bring it to a halt. The Qing [Ch'ing] dynasty that replaced it was established by a Tatar tribe called Manchu and lasted from 1644 to 1911 under ten emperors who ruled from the Forbidden City in Beijing. The Manchu were related to the earlier Tatar tribe, the Nüchen, who had betrayed Song Huizong in 1127 when they took away the northern half of his empire and established the Jin dynasty. Both of these Tatar tribes came from the forested regions in northern Manchuria. In the late sixteenth century, the Manchu had emerged into literacy with the invention of a writing system. By 1616, when rival groups were united under a chieftain named Nurhachi, they had become a kingdom bent on conquest. Nurhachi's son, Abahai (r. 1627–1643), set his sights on the Ming empire. He succeeded in conquering the areas north of the Great Wall that were under Ming control, and in 1636 he declared himself first emperor of the Qing ("Pure") dynasty. With the help of treacherous rebelling factions within the Ming empire, his forces took Beijing in 1644. The last Ming emperor hung himself in the

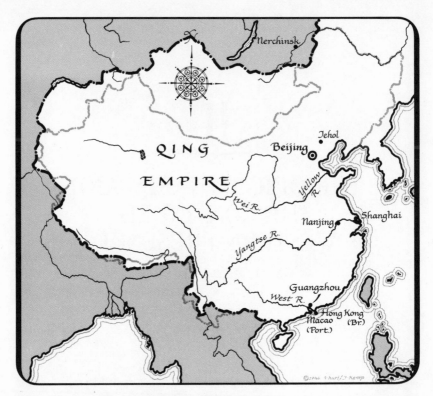

Qing Dynasty Empire (1644–1911)

imperial palace on April 3, but Abahai, who had died a few months earlier, did not live to enjoy his ultimate triumph. Instead, his heir, a seven-year-old nephew, became the first Qing emperor to rule from Beijing.

More than the Mongols of the Yuan dynasty, the Manchu were successful in adapting to and assimilating Chinese culture and in preserving the Ming form of government; they won over rebellious generals and officials with offers of high positions. They ruled with the help of Manchu forces divided into companies known as "banners," military units that marched under banners of different colors. These were headed by Tatar generals who were higher in rank than their civil counterparts and therefore independent of them. The banner troops were placed strategically throughout the empire and had no other job than to keep the peace while living on pensions. Eventually, they would prove an enormous drain on the Qing government and a useless one.

One of the most detested impositions of foreign rule was the Manchu custom requiring Chinese men to shave the front of their heads and wear the rest of their hair in a pigtail, or queue. The Chinese style, from at least the time of the third century B.C., and documented by clay tomb figures, relief carvings, and paintings of the Qin and later dynasties, was for a man to wear his hair in a topknot often covered under a cap shaped to accommodate it. Under the Manchu, topknots were forbidden. Exceptions were made only for Taoist priests, who were allowed to keep the traditional topknot, and for Buddhist monks, who could shave their heads completely.

The Kangxi [K'ang-hsi] Emperor

The Kangxi emperor, known best by his reign name (which means "Lasting Peace"), was the second Qing monarch and succeeded his father, Abahai's nephew, in 1661. The father had died of smallpox at the age of twenty-four, and the son was only seven years old when he ascended the throne. But, by the age of thirteen, he insisted on ruling without regents.

His reign was the longest in Chinese history, lasting from 1661 to 1722. He was a contemporary of Louis XIV of France, with whom he corresponded, and of Peter the Great of Russia, with whom he negotiated a treaty. This treaty, signed in 1689 at Nerchinsk, divided up Manchuria between the Russians and the Chinese. The Chinese delegation sent to negotiate it included a Jesuit priest, Father Gerbillon. He is considered largely responsible for the outcome of the negotiations, in part because he acted as translator, speaking Latin to the Russians and Chinese to the Manchu. One wonders how much either side understood because this treaty would, in our own time, nearly cause a war, and the two nations are still arguing today over the exact location of that boundary.

The Kangxi emperor extended the borders of the empire to the north and west, at times leading his forces himself. With the help of the banner guard, he kept the peace within those borders. He climbed Tai Shan, in Shandong province, the most sacred of five mountains considered sacred Daoist sites; he visited the tomb of Confucius at Qufu, also in Shandong; he had a dictionary of over

Figure 46. The Manchu emperors adopted the traditional Chinese dragon robe but outlawed the wearing of topknots. The Kangxi emperor wears a fur-brimmed hat with a pearl set in gold at the top. The Metropolitan Museum of Art, gift of Mrs. Edward S. Harkness, 1947

eighty thousand Chinese characters compiled; in sum, he worked incessantly to assimilate Chinese culture into his own life and rule. Despite his Manchu blood, he tried to be a model Confucian ruler.

The issue of Christianity surfaced particularly during the Kangxi reign. Christianity had been proscribed off and on during the seventeenth century, but the assistance of Father Gerbillon in negotiating the Treaty of Nerchinsk, together with what were perceived as Jesuit contributions in the sciences, persuaded the

Kangxi emperor that Christianity was not harmful and could be preached to his subjects. However, in 1715 the Catholic Church, in a letter from the Pope to the emperor, demanded that Christian Chinese must not continue the Confucian rituals of ancestor worship. The Kangxi emperor was outraged by this interference with his authority and forbade the further teaching of the Christian religion in China.

The Kangxi emperor died of a cold in 1722 at the age of sixty-eight. He had established a stable dynasty that survived, despite constant internal and external pressures, into the twentieth century.

His most noteworthy successor, the Qianlong [Ch'ien-lung] emperor (1736–1796), expanded the empire to its greatest size. Territories in Central Asia, Mongolia, and Tibet all became part of his dominions. (The Central Asian territory is present-day Xinjiang Uygur province; Inner Mongolia and Tibet are still autonomous regions of the People's Republic of China.) The Qianlong emperor was a Confucian devotee, a great patron of the arts, a builder of palaces—his reign saw the zenith of Qing rule.

A famous Chinese literary work of the mid-eighteenth century, generally considered the greatest of Chinese novels, is a tragic love story that provides a panoramic view of society under the Qianlong emperor. *The Dream of the Red Chamber* (also translated as *The Romance of the Stone*) by Cao Xueqin [Ts'ao Hsüeh-ch'in] is beautifully written, Tolstoyan in scope, and tells us much about the internal relationships and priorities of Chinese families. The hero, a young man of educated background, must pass his examinations, become a successful scholar-official, and marry not for love but for duty so that he can arrest the decline of his family's position and fortune. All other things are secondary to this goal. The author's genius is revealed in his moving delineation of the tensions between duty and desire in the life of his hero. The story was not only in part the author's own but was also repeated countless times in the society of his day. Families often slaved for generations to save the money needed to support an aspiring scholar. Their reward came, sometimes posthumously, when a successful degree candidate was granted the additional privilege of extending his newly won status to his ancestors, who thereby became enrolled in the exalted ranks of the educated.

The scholar class was unquestionably the most prestigious of the four traditional classes in China. This was true even though scholars often did not have great wealth. The members of the other three classes, the peasants, the artisans, and the merchants, were considered commoners. The peasants, honored as providers of the most basic necessity, food, were next in social rank but, in fact, often lived just above starvation level. In contrast, the merchants, even when they had great wealth, were at the bottom of the social ladder; the artisans fell somewhere in between. By the late eighteenth century, Qing rule had deteriorated. The earlier expansion of the empire under the Qianlong emperor and the ensuing prosperity that it brought fostered an enormous increase in population, especially among the lower classes. Fewer and fewer could aspire to raise their status, and many of those who had belonged to the bureaucracy sank into poverty. The inevitable clashes between the rich and poor were settled more often than not by military intervention. This time, however, dynastic decline was complicated by a new factor: the growing presence of Europeans.

The West Moves in on the Middle Kingdom: Stage One
1644–1800

The Western traders who had arrived at Guangzhou in the first half of the seventeenth century continued to press for the easing of trade restrictions. The Manchu began by allowing the establishment of trading posts, or hongs, downriver from Guangzhou. Each Western nation was assigned and flew its flag over a hong which was run by Chinese members of an official merchant guild. They dictated the trade arrangements as well as the management of the hong. No women were allowed in the hong, not even as servants. Westerners were forbidden to learn Chinese; instead the

*Figure 47. A view of hongs, or trading posts, in Guangzhou decorates
a lacquered tray made for the American market in the early nineteenth
century.* The Metropolitan Museum of Art, Rogers Fund, 1941

Chinese merchants spoke pidgin English, French, Dutch, etc. The
Westerners were considered violent barbarians: The fair- or red-
headed Dutch and English were "red-haired devils"; Americans
were "flowery-flag devils" because of the stars and stripes of the
flag that flew over their hong.

The Chinese allowed no other trade arrangements or ports. In
1793 King George III of England, newly stripped of his American
colonies, sought more favorable trading arrangements with China.
He sent a formal embassy, led by the Irishman Lord Macartney,
to the aged Qianlong emperor. Three ships carrying a suitable
retinue of men and a collection of impressive gifts sailed upriver
to Beijing, only to discover that the emperor was summering at
Jehol, one of his seventy vacation palaces. Lord Macartney left
some of the larger gifts in Beijing and proceeded on to Jehol. The
gifts included a planetarium, a telescope, ship models, six light
cannons on wheels, and a coach with gilt carvings, glass windows,
springs, and velvet seats. This latter caused great consternation

117

Figure 48. Lord Macartney's reception by the Qianlong emperor, in 1793, was recorded in pen and ink by William Alexander at the Chinese court. Courtesy of the British Library

among the Manchu and Chinese officials because the coachman's seat was placed higher than the emperor's. The coachman's seat was promptly lowered.

In arranging for an audience with the emperor, a delicate matter of etiquette had to be settled. The Chinese custom, adopted by the Manchu, required that those who appeared before the emperor kowtow. They were to kneel on both knees and touch their foreheads to the ground three times. Lord Macartney considered this unacceptable. He would kneel on both knees only before God. To his king he would kneel on one knee while kissing his sovereign's ringed hand. This is what he insisted on doing before the eighty-three-year-old Qianlong emperor, and this is what the Manchu finally agreed upon.

After this initial ceremony, at which Lord Macartney presented King George's written request for better trade arrangements and a British embassy in Beijing, there followed banquets and gift presentations. The English were entertained on hunting expeditions, and finally Lord Macartney was given the emperor's reply to take back to the English court. This, in part, is what King George read:

The celestial Empire possesses all things in prolific abundance and lacks no product within its borders. There is therefore no need to import the manufactures of outside barbarians in exchange for our own products.

As for an embassy:

. . . any European living in Peking is forbidden to leave the empire or write to his country. . . .[1]

An embassy, therefore, would serve no purpose.

The West Moves in on the Middle Kingdom: The Opium Wars and the First Unequal Treaties
1800–1876

In the late eighteenth century, British imports of Chinese tea were six times greater than its exports to China, mostly cotton goods and spices. In an attempt to overcome this imbalance, the English encouraged the exportation of opium produced in British-ruled India to the Chinese. In 1815, as ever larger numbers of Chinese and Manchu alike spent more money and time on the drug, the Qing government officially banned its import. The British bribed the Qing officials who searched their ships and continued to smuggle the drug in exchange for silver coin. Ultimately the imbalance was reversed in favor of the British, and it was now the Qing treasury that was drained of silver.

The Qing government passed further laws making the import and smoking of opium illegal. A great scholar-official, Lin Zexu [Lin Tze-hsu], who had been governor-general of Hunan and Hubei provinces, was made commissioner in charge of enforcing these

1. Elizabeth Seeger, *The Pageant of Chinese History* (London: Longmans, Green and Co. Ltd, 1934), 322.

laws. In an appeal to Queen Victoria (which probably never reached her), he wrote:

> The ways of God are without partiality; it is not permissible to injure another in order to profit oneself . . . is there any single article from China which has done any harm to foreign countries? Take tea and rhubarb, for example; foreign countries cannot get along for a single day without them. . . . On the other hand, articles coming from outside to China can only be used as toys. . . . There is, however, a class of treacherous barbarians who manufacture opium, smuggle it in for sale, and deceive our foolish people. . . . Not to smoke yourselves, but yet to dare to prepare and sell to and beguile the foolish masses of the Middle Kingdom is to protect one's own life while leading others to death, to gather profit for oneself while bringing injury upon others. . . . I now propose that we shall unite to put a final stop to this curse of opium. . . .[2]

This rational appeal certainly ran counter to the interests of both the English and the Chinese and Manchu who were profiting from the opium business. When, in 1839, Commissioner Lin seized twenty thousand chests of opium, burned them on the beach near Guangzhou, and formally apologized to the sea for this pollution, the British declared war.

The first Opium War lasted for three years. The British soundly defeated the Chinese with superior weapons. The Treaty of Nanjing, signed in 1842, was the first of a series of treaties now referred to by historians as "unequal treaties" because the Manchu were forced to give in to Western demands while receiving little in return. In this first case, Hong Kong was ceded to Britain, five trading ports were opened to British consulates with all tariffs to be fixed by mutual agreement, and a huge indemnity of twenty-

---

2. Lin Zexu, transl. in H. A. Giles, *Gems of Chinese Literature* (New York: Paragon Book Reprint Corp., 1965), 265–267.

one million silver dollars was exacted from the Chinese by the British.

The Chinese were forced to sign other such unequal treaties with the United States (the Treaty of Wanghia) and with France (the Treaty of Huangpu [Whampoa]), both in 1844. Britain maintained a most-favored-nation status.

The Chinese were forced to relinquish the view, held over so many millennia, that their kingdom was the middle, or central, kingdom, with an empire that included "all that was under Heaven." It was a painful entrance into world politics.

The second Opium War (1856–1858) was a repeat of the first. As the Western powers continued the smuggling of opium and the demands for even greater trading advantages, the Chinese government tried to resist Western pressure. Then, in 1856, Chinese officers boarded a Chinese boat sailing under a British captain at Guangzhou and arrested the crew on charges of piracy. This set off the second war between the Chinese and the British, who were backed by the French.

Again the Western forces beat the Chinese. In 1858 another unequal treaty, the Treaty of Tianjin [Tien-tsin], was drawn up. This made allowances for opium trade, missionary activity, more trading ports and benefits to the Westerners, and at long last, consulates were permitted in Beijing. The Manchu found it hard to agree to this treaty and were hostile to Western envoys sent to the Qing court in Beijing to observe its ratification. As a result, Anglo-French forces attacked Beijing and burned down the Summer Palace, a great treasure-house of Chinese art outside the city. The Manchu ratified the treaty and gave in to the further demand, formalized in the Treaty of Beijing of 1860, that foreign embassies be allowed in the capital.

Taiping [T'ai-ping] Rebellion

As though the Western powers were not enough of a plague to the Manchu court, rebellion from within, that chronic sign of the crumbling rule of a dynasty, came close to destroying Manchu power. The rebellion began in the 1840s. The leader was a missionary-taught schoolmaster, Hong Xiuquan [Hung Hsiu-ch'uan] (1814–1864), whose readings in Protestant texts inspired him to believe he had received the Mandate of Heaven to save his people. He found a ready following among the peasants, who were oppressed by both landlords and the Manchu taxes, which were increased in the 1840s to pay for the Opium Wars and the indemnities imposed by the unequal treaties.

Hong Xiuquan preached an astounding egalitarian message: "All men under heaven are brothers, and all women are sisters." This was anathema to the orthodox Confucian model of a preordained social hierarchy. He promised a society, the Heavenly Kingdom of Taiping ("Great Peace"), where justice prevailed, land was evenly distributed, and monogamy replaced the concubine system. Hong Xiuquan declared himself Heavenly King. By 1851 the Taiping army had captured large areas in the southern half of the empire, and two years later it took Nanjing, which was renamed Tianjing [T'ien-ching] ("Heavenly Capital"). Hong Xiuquan announced his plan for the Heavenly Land System, which called for the division of land into equal shares for all persons of both sexes above the age of sixteen, with half shares to those younger.

Hong Xiuquan's reforms differed sharply from those of Wang Mang, of the first century, and Wang Anshi, of the eleventh. These men had advocated adjustments in a hierarchical society ruled by a centralized imperial government. Hong Xiuquan, in contrast, proposed the communal sharing of land, food, clothing, and money among every member of a society organized into units of twenty-five households each. The aged or disabled would be supported by their unit. Everyone had a right to an education, and women as well as men could serve in the government and the army.

Equality for women was among the most revolutionary of these ideas. Since the disappearance of prehistoric matriarchies, women had been inferiors in China. As daughters, they were neglected in favor of sons. As wives or concubines, they owed unswerving obedience to their husbands or lovers and were not allowed to own anything in their own right. Since at least the eleventh century, they had endured bound feet. In the few cases when women acquired power, their role was inevitably seen as destructive. Although bound feet were outlawed under the Taiping regime, the custom did not die out until the mid-twentieth century, and it was only then that women were given the legal right to own property and choose their husbands.

As with the programs of Wang Mang and Wang Anshi, the Taiping program, while unsuccessful in its own time, planted the seeds for the future, seeds that would take root a hundred years later. Then the ideas of Hong Xiuquan, combined with those of his European contemporary Karl Marx, would shape the People's Republic of China.

Between 1855 and 1865, it took the concerted effort of the Manchu armies and the British and French forces to finally suppress the Taipings. Even then, although Hong Xiuquan had committed suicide in 1864, during the prolonged battle for his capital, splinter groups fought on until 1876.

The West Moves in
on the Middle Kingdom:
The Boxer Rebellion and the
Last Unequal Treaty
1899–1901

The Boxers, Yi He Quan [I-ho Ch'üan] ("Society of the Righteous and Harmonious Fist"), were a secret order who sought reform of the Manchu rule. They also resented the growing presence of Westerners in China, a sentiment shared by a large portion of the population. In 1899 the granting of special privileges and powers by the Manchu to Roman Catholics provoked an attack by a section of the Yi He Quan on churches and missionaries. The Qing forces were unable to suppress this uprising, which soon grew into a widespread rebellion. While the Western powers pressed the Qing to suppress the Yi He Quan, the empress dowager Cixi (see below) plotted to use the Yi He Quan to her own ends. Her secret hope was to rout the Westerners from Beijing. Cixi encouraged the Yi He Quan army to enter Beijing, where they soon had the foreign quarters under siege. In June 1900 Britain, Russia, Japan, the United States, Germany, France, Italy, and Austria combined

Figure 49. Boxer prisoners are guarded by soldiers of the Sixth United States Cavalry, Tianjin, 1901. Library of Congress

forces, and after initial defeats, succeeded in occupying Beijing by August. This set the stage for the next unequal treaty, the International Protocol of 1901. Among other things, it exacted further enormous indemnities from China. In return for backing the two-faced rule of the Qing under the empress dowager, the Western powers gained a free hand for their trading and missionary interests and increased residential privileges for their nationals. The Middle Kingdom was now under de facto colonial rule.

The Empress Dowager Cixi [Ts'u-hsi]

Cixi, the last effective ruler of the Qing dynasty, who ruled in fact if not in name from 1861 to 1908, started as the favorite concubine of the Xianfeng [Hsien-feng] emperor. When he died in 1861, and

Figure 50. A company of the Bengal Lancers escorts Count Alfred von Waldersee, supreme commander of the Allied forces that helped to suppress the Boxer Rebellion, to the Meridian Gate of the Forbidden City. The Westerners gained yet more concessions from the Qing government. Library of Congress

her infant son became the Tongzhi [T'ung-chih] emperor, she came to power as coregent with the widowed empress. This lady was no match for Cixi, who in effect ruled the empire for the next forty-seven years. When the Tongzhi emperor died, Cixi replaced him with her nephew, the Guangxu [Kuang-hsu] emperor, and made herself regent.

It is said that she ruled with iron-willed cruelty and vindictiveness and flew into monumental rages that literally caused heads to roll. After a day of such exertions, she calmed her nerves by puffing on an opium pipe—only in moderation, however. Her real addiction was to power.

When, in 1898, Cixi's nephew, the emperor, tried to effect

125

Figure 51. This beguiling young woman bore an imperial son and became the formidable empress dowager, Cixi (1835–1911). New York Public Library Picture Collection

reforms—during what is known as the Hundred Days' Reform—and to remove her from power, she put him under guard, where he stayed for the last ten years of his life; she executed those of his co-reformers who had not fled. Her conservatism, so ruthlessly maintained, prevented any modernization of Chinese society or the use of its resources. She put Manchu dominance and her own rule first and saw no need to consider the needs or aspirations of her Chinese subjects.

"I prefer to give China to the foreigners rather than to surrender it to my own slaves," she once said.[3] In this she referred, in part, to the court eunuchs, all of whom were Chinese because castration was forbidden to men of Manchu blood. When she first came to the harem, they had been her informants on court life. After her

3. Cixi, quoted in Dun J. Li, *The Ageless Chinese* (New York: Charles Scribner's Sons, 1978), 414.

Figure 52. In this 1903 photograph taken aboard the imperial barge, Cixi poses as the Buddhist goddess of mercy behind lotus blossoms. The chief eunuch, on her left, and another on her right are dressed as her divine attendants. Courtesy of the Freer Gallery of Art, Smithsonian Institution, Washington, D.C.

rise to power, they became her agents. Her chief eunuch, Li Lianying [Li Lien-ying], was her principal confidant and used his office to acquire a fortune in bribes from those seeking favors from the empress dowager. He was also her companion at court entertainments—more often than not held in her newly rebuilt Summer Palace outside Beijing—for which she dressed herself as the Buddhist goddess of mercy and he became her divine attendant. It was under the rule of such as these that China entered the twentieth century.

12

REVOLUTION:
THE UPHILL CLIMB

1911–1919

Because they are so close to us, the events of this century require more detailed scrutiny than any previously described. However, to follow them is like tracing the complex strands of a Chinese knot.

At the beginning of the twentieth century, we are confronted with the destructive rule of the Qing empress dowager Cixi, the humiliating dominance of the Western powers, the abject failure of several attempts by the Chinese to revolt or win reforms, and the general feeling among many Chinese that they must reclaim sovereignty of the Middle Kingdom for themselves. Today's People's Republic of China attests to the extraordinary success of that reclamation effort. How did it happen?

One way to tell the story is to follow the lives of the three principal Chinese leaders of the century: Sun Yat-sen, Chiang Kai-shek, and Mao Zedong.

Sun Yat-sen [pinyin: Sun Zhongshan]

Sun Yat-sen (1866–1925) was the son of a peasant living in Guangdong province on the mainland near Macao, an area far from the capital and one that had known Western traders since the seventeenth century; many of its privileged young men had studied

128

Figure 53. Students in Beijing demonstrate against the Treaty of Versailles, May 4, 1919. New York Public Library Picture Collection

and lived abroad. Sun's uncle, who had fought for the Taiping Rebellion, was his first teacher, and Hong Xiuquan was Sun's hero. When Sun was thirteen, he was sent to Honolulu to join his older brother; there he attended an Anglican mission school for three years and was baptized a Christian. (Hawaii was then an independent monarchy; it became a United States territory in 1900.) He returned home, found he could not tolerate the traditional ways, and with financial support from his brother in Honolulu—now a successful businessman—he went to Guangzhou and Hong Kong to study medicine. Sun was impressed by the contrast between these two cities: Guangzhou was overcrowded, disease-ridden, and filthy while across the bay, British-developed Hong Kong was clean, orderly, and modern. His early admiration for the leader of the Taiping Rebellion, who had sought to bring Western ideas to Chinese society, became a fervent determination to continue the effort to modernize China.

In 1892 Sun received a medical degree from a British mission

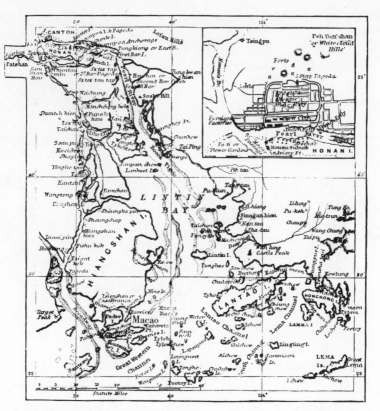

Guangzhou (Canton) Area, Late Nineteenth Century

Guangzhou and surrounding area in the late nineteenth century, showing mouth of Pearl River, Hong Kong, and Macao. From S. Wells Williams, *The Middle Kingdom*, 1893.

hospital, but when he tried to practice medicine in Macao, the Portuguese colony, he was stopped because he had no Portuguese medical credentials. He then went to practice in Guangzhou, where he met young patriots who reinforced his growing belief in the need for revolution against the Qing rule. In 1894 he went back to Honolulu, where he started a revolutionary society among overseas Chinese called Xing Zhong Hui [Hsing-chung Hui] ("Society for the Revival of China"). Then, in 1895, he returned to China and set up the society's headquarters in Hong Kong. Sun Yat-sen had given up medicine and become a professional revolutionary. He continued to travel back and forth between South China and Honolulu, and later Japan, the United States, and Europe, in order

Figure 54. Guangzhou's crowded floating homes and poverty dismayed Sun Yat-sen. Library of Congress

Figure 55. A view of Hong Kong as seen from the Peak in 1900. Library of Congress

to coordinate political and financial support among Chinese living overseas for a revolution on the mainland.

His initial attempt at revolution took place in 1895, when Sun and his followers plotted to seize the government offices in Guangzhou. This was to be the first step in an armed uprising. But the plot was discovered, and although Sun managed to escape to Japan, forty-six of his co-conspirators were executed.

In Japan, Sun carried out a personal rebellion against Qing rule: He cut off his queue, adopted Western dress, and grew a mustache. Since he was now wanted by the Qing government, this change of style also provided a disguise, which he completed by taking an alias while he remained in Japan. He moved on to Honolulu, the United States, and England, still seeking support for his cause.

In October 1896, Dr. Sun arrived in London, where he met Dr. James Cantlie, one of the English doctors who had trained him in Hong Kong. Soon after settling into lodgings in London, Dr. Sun was kidnapped and held prisoner in a room at the top of the Chinese embassy and told that he would be deported to China and executed. Dr. Sun dropped messages out the window of his room, but no one picked them up. Finally he got word through one of his warders to Dr. Cantlie that he was being held under threat of deportation and death. Dr. Cantlie went to the police, to Scotland Yard, and to the *London Times*, all to no avail. No one believed him. Dr. Cantlie had detectives watch the Chinese embassy while he and a colleague went to the courts in the Old Bailey to seek other legal means to save Dr. Sun. The story was picked up at the Old Bailey by a *Globe* reporter, and on October 24 the story of Dr. Sun's kidnapping broke in the paper's headlines. Soon the news spread around the world, and Dr. Sun was freed. At age thirty, he became an international celebrity who was seen as *the* leader of Chinese revolt against the Qing rule.

During the rest of his stay in England, Dr. Sun spent much time in the British Museum's reading room, as had many other revolutionaries before him, including Marx, studying English and French political thinkers, philosophers, and economists. He is not known to have read Marx. He based his revolutionary doctrine on what he called the Three People's Principles: the People's Race (restore China to the Chinese), the People's Rights (establish constitutional democracy), and the People's Livelihood (guarantee fair distribution of land and wealth). Dr. Sun compared these to Abraham Lincoln's "of the people, by the people, and for the people."

Sun Yat-sen traveled in Europe and Japan to mobilize groups of young Chinese studying abroad in support of his revolution. Meanwhile others in China were working to resist or at least change Qing policies, but without success.

Eventually, in Japan in 1905, the several exiled Chinese rebel groups got together and became the Tong Meng Hui [T'ung-meng Hui] ("United League"), with Sun Yat-sen as leader. The league had a paper, the *People's Journal*, which became the voice of the revolutionary movement. The first issue carried a manifesto by Sun Yat-sen introducing the Three People's Principles. Between 1906 and 1908, the United League led a series of uprisings in South China with Sun Yat-sen personally participating in one in Guangxi province. But, once again, these failed to overthrow Qing rule.

Meanwhile, in the capital in 1908, the empress dowager sensed her dying day approaching, and, vindictive and controlling to the end, she arranged for the emperor's death on the day before she herself was to die, designating his brother as regent and the brother's two-year-old son as the new emperor. The new regent was forceful enough at the start of his tenure to persuade the empress's military strongman to resign. (This was Yuan Shikai [Yuan Shih-k'ai], the Chinese general who had saved the empress dowager from the Hundred Days' Reform plot and who had developed a model army to protect her. However, as we shall see, this was not the end of Yuan Shikai.) The regent decreed an imperial constitution, and during the next two years, the provinces set up their own councils, and the government's army was recruited from local peasants—who, as it turned out, were frequently more loyal to rebellious uprisers than to the Qing emperor.

What brought things to a head in 1911, the year of the revolution? What was the spark that finally set off an uprising big enough to end the Manchu rule?

The empress dowager was dead, and her replacement, although he seemed less offensive than she had been, was, by the same token, ineffectual. The presence of the Western powers was still strong. For them, China was a gold mine of opportunity. China had cheap labor for new industries, but better yet, the industries required transportation, transportation required railroads, and railroads were a good investment. It was a fight over a railroad which brought the nationalist Chinese spirit to the point of explosion.

The railroad in dispute was the line being built between Sichuan province, one of the most populous and fertile provinces, and the large industrial center of Wuhan, in Hubei province. The provincial councils had raised money to build this line by selling shares to the population as a forced tax. However, the Qing government wanted control of this railroad as an important link in the imperial network, and in May 1911 the government announced that it had obtained a loan from a consortium of Western powers to take over and build this line, nationalizing it, as it were. The word *nationalizing* was a travesty in this context, because to the Chinese in Sichuan and Hubei, provincial ownership of the railway was a source of true Chinese pride, while for the Qing to take over the line was a further sign of Manchu domination and a move backed by and ultimately profitable to Western imperialist powers.

Fighting broke out between local Sichuan militia and government forces. Then, on October 9, 1911, the long-smoldering rebellion burst into a roaring flame when a bomb exploded in the revolutionary headquarters in Wuhan. The next day, the police, alerted to the insurgents, imprisoned and beheaded people indiscriminately. (October 10 is celebrated as a national holiday, the Double Ten, the tenth day of the tenth month.) The government army units in Wuhan rebelled and joined the revolutionaries, and together these forces took over Wuhan. On October 22 Hubei province declared itself independent of Beijing. By the end of November, fifteen of China's eighteen provinces had joined the revolution. In desperation, the Qing government begged Yuan Shikai to come out of retirement with his model army and put down the revolution. Yuan Shikai agreed to try, on the condition that he be made premier and commander-in-chief of the military. But he didn't try too hard. He went only so far as to keep the revolution out of the capital and waited for the smoke to clear while he plotted his route to the top.

Meanwhile Sun Yat-sen was in the United States lecturing and fund raising. When he learned of the October Wuhan uprising, he went to London and then to Japan, lobbying to prevent foreign intervention against the revolution. Then he came to Nanjing, where, on December 29, 1911, the representatives of seventeen provinces met and elected him provisional president of the newly declared Republic of China, or Zhonghua Minguo [Chung-hua Min-kuo]. But it soon became clear that a devastating civil war would be inevitable unless a deal was made with the northern strongman, Yuan Shikai, and his puppet, the child emperor. After a month of wily negotiations, Yuan Shikai made his next move: He promised to give military support to the new republic and see that the emperor abdicated in exchange for the position of provisional president held by Dr. Sun. Sun Yat-sen accepted these conditions; they seemed the only way to prevent further fighting.

Thus it was that on February 12, 1912, the Manchu rule of China ended in the abdication of the child emperor. Even more important, this date marked the end of more than three-and-one-half millennia of dynastic rule in China.

Yuan Shikai was not willing to see dynastic rule die forever and, before long, made a scurrilous attempt to place himself on the throne. At first, he allowed the ex–child emperor to live on in the Forbidden City as a guest of the state, keeping the throne warm, as it were, for his own eventual use. (This unfortunate child's career as a puppet did not end here: He was put back up on the throne in Beijing in 1917 for a twelve-day stint as emperor, and later the Japanese installed him as emperor of Manchukuo in 1932. Finally, after imprisonment under both Russians and Chinese, he lived out his old age as Henry Pu Yi, a reeducated comrade of the People's Republic of China.) As provisional president of a parliamentary democracy, Yuan Shikai arranged the assassination of the key figures in the Guomindang [Kuomintang] ("Nationalist Party") which Dr. Sun had started in August 1912. Dr. Sun escaped and organized a "second revolution" in 1913. Yuan Shikai suppressed this in turn, dismissed the parliament, declared himself president for life in May 1914 and, finally, emperor of a new dynasty in December 1915.

This travesty was greeted by revolt all over China and the

135

eventual withdrawal of the foreign support which had encouraged it. Exhausted and defeated by his own scheming, Yuan Shikai died in June 1916.

He set an example, however, for a group of military strongmen, commonly called warlords, who kept China—especially the northern half—in turmoil from the time of his death until the late twenties. These men used mercenary armies to capture villages, provinces, railroads—in short, anything that would give them a power base. They had no political rallying cry; they were interested in the local peasants only as suppliers of provisions for their troops. The peasants, in turn, saw little difference between one ravaging army and another and despised them all equally. The warlords' only aim was crude power, and unlike Yuan Shikai (or the much earlier contenders for the Three Kingdoms, who are sometimes referred to as warlords), they did not attempt to start dynasties. Small warlords—and there were hundreds of them from every level of society—joined behind big ones. The most successful were men trained under Yuan Shikai himself. Several of these, one after the other, seized control of the parliamentary government in Beijing, reinstalled after Yuan Shikai's death, but none succeeded in holding it for more than a few years, nor did any of them dominate anything close to all of China. They resorted to any means, whether armed force, government office, political maneuvering—such as reinstalling the child emperor on the throne—or alliances with Japan, to prolong their brief tenures. None proposed any program of reform or political change in any way comparable to that of Sun Yat-sen. He, in contrast, had a political vision but never the means to make it a reality.

Sun Yat-sen, during the years before and after Yuan Shikai's death, traveled back and forth between Japan and South China, endlessly creating and coordinating groups of followers. In Guangzhou, in 1917, he resorted to warlord strategy and declared himself the generalissimo at the head of a military government. But even then he could not create a real power base. The path of his career begins to recede into the background somewhat as that of his disciple Chiang Kai-shek comes to the fore. One event must be noted, however, before we pick up Chiang Kai-shek's trail. While

Dr. Sun was in Tokyo in 1915, he was divorced from his first wife and, at forty-nine, married Soong Ching-ling, the beautiful American-educated second daughter of one of his most faithful financial backers. Twenty-six years his junior, she had just replaced her older sister as his personal secretary. In view of the later history of this family, this marriage was significant. Ching-ling's younger sister married Dr. Sun's protégé, Chiang Kai-shek, in 1927 and became the well-known friend of F.D.R. and other important Americans, while her brother, T. V. Soong, became one of Chiang Kai-shek's closest colleagues. In the later confrontation between Chiang Kai-shek and Mao Zedong, Ching-ling—called both Mme. Sun Yat-sen and Mme. Soong—sided with the Communists. They rewarded her, when they came to power, by giving her a splendid home in Beijing, where she lived as a revered figure. Shortly before her death in 1981, she was made an honorary president of China.

Chiang Kai-shek [pinyin: *Jiang Jieshi*]

Chiang Kai-shek (we will use the more familiar romanization) was born in 1887 in Zhejiang province, the son of a salt merchant who died when the boy was eight. Chiang's mother was a devout Buddhist and a strict disciplinarian. The boy was tutored from the age of four in the study of the Confucian classics. His first marriage was arranged when he was fourteen, and at seventeen he studied at a local school called the Pavilion of Literature. The works of Song dynasty militarists advocating a Spartan life-style and high moral aims impressed him, as did Sun Yat-sen's burgeoning revolutionary movement. Chiang decided to pursue both a military career and the cause of revolution and saw Japan as the best place to accomplish his aims. His family tried to dissuade him, but he changed their minds by cutting off his queue. By the standards of his time, this made him a rebel who was better off away from home.

Though he was not accepted at the military academy in Tokyo, he did meet some of Sun Yat-sen's disciples. He returned to China, was accepted there into the Baoding Military Academy, where he excelled, and was sent back to Japan to continue his military

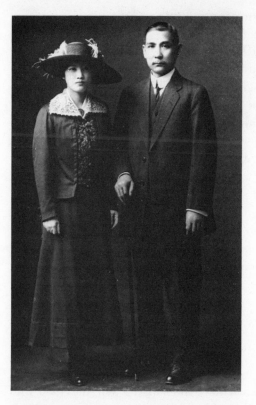

Figure 56. Dr. Sun Yat-sen with his second wife, Soong Ching-ling, in Japan, 1915. New China Pictures Co.

studies. In Tokyo in 1908, he met and spoke with Sun Yat-sen at a meeting of the United League and pledged his allegiance to the revolutionary cause. When he heard of the October 10, 1911, explosion in Wuhan, he left Tokyo and rushed to the scene of action, where he distinguished himself as the leader of an attack on the governor's office. When Yuan Shikai's regime took over, he returned once again to Tokyo and to further military studies, but in 1913 he was back in China, a key participant in the unsuccessful "second revolution" and an admiring friend to Sun Yat-sen, who, though defeated once again, was still determined to make a reality of the Three People's Principles. For the next several years, Chiang Kai-shek was based in Shanghai, where he cemented ties established earlier with a notorious group called the Green Gang. During this time, his activities and associations were often more criminal than revolutionary. In 1917 Sun Yat-sen declared a National Military Government in Guangzhou and invited Chiang Kai-shek to be his personal lieutenant. From this position, Chiang moved steadily upward in Guomindang power until, ten years later, and two years after Dr. Sun's death, he succeeded in establishing a tenuous control over China under the military regime called the Republic of China, with a capital in Nanjing.

May 4, 1919

The date marks the emergence of a new group in China's struggle: student demonstrators. Their actions have increasingly been credited with changing the course of the Chinese revolution. As background, we must look to the events both outside and inside China from 1914 to 1919. In Europe, World War I began in August 1914. China, under Yuan Shikai, immediately declared neutrality. Japan, however, joined the Allied forces and declared war on Germany. She then seized the province of Shandong, where Germany had commercial concessions, and claimed these for herself. This was Japan's first step in what was to be a thirty-year effort, ultimately unsuccessful, to colonize China. Japan had been preparing for this for a long time. In 1895 she defeated the Qing armies under the leadership of Yuan Shikai, no less, and took part of Korea as well as the island of Formosa (Taiwan). She further consolidated this position when conflict with Russia, over control of North Korea and Russian-built Manchurian railways, was settled in 1905. The treaty negotiated at that time, through the efforts of President Theodore Roosevelt, gave Japan undisputed control of all Korea and of a major portion of the Manchurian railways. The Chinese were reinstated, on paper at least, as administrative rulers of Manchuria. It was nine years after this that Japan invaded Shandong. Her next move, in 1915, was to send a secret document, listing twenty-one demands, to Yuan Shikai. These pressed for virtual colonization of China in exchange for support of Yuan Shikai's presidency. Yuan Shikai, ever the opportunist, made the best of the situation and, to the horror and dismay of most of his fellow Chinese, gave in to the Japanese demands. But he insisted that he remain the uncontested ruler of China, an ambition that, as we have seen, he was unable to realize.

Meanwhile a new intellectual movement was taking place in

Shanghai. There a magazine, *New Youth*, edited by a key figure in this movement, Chen Duxiu [Ch'en Tu-hsiu], became the forum for the discussion of democracy, education, equality of the sexes, and an empirical approach to scientific inquiry. The work of Lu Xun [Lu Hsün], a prominent figure in modern Chinese literature (and possibly the best known internationally), first appeared in these pages. His stories have been compared to those of Gogol and Chekhov; they held up a mocking mirror to traditional Chinese customs. His most famous, "Diary of a Madman," is a satirical account of a madman convinced that between the lines of traditional Chinese writings he sees the words "Eat men!"

Between 1917 and 1919, this movement was brought to Beijing. Chen Duxiu became a dean and Lu Xun a professor at the University of Beijing, an institution founded at the turn of the century and modeled after Western universities. Here Chen Duxiu and others of the new intelligentsia taught a generation of students to plot, not in the traditional manner of secret societies, but in the sanctioned classrooms of a national university; to plot a new era for China freed from the conservative, backward-looking yoke of Confucian traditions and from the manipulative stranglehold of foreigners.

In Europe in the spring of 1919, World War I was over, and the Versailles Conference convened to negotiate a peace treaty. The French and British backed Japan's claims to the German interests in Shandong, and the United States, which at first promised to support the Chinese against the Japanese, yielded to Japan's demands.

The Versailles Conference was closely followed in China, especially in Beijing. There control of the official Chinese government was, for the moment, in the hands of one of the warlord factions known as the Anhui clique. This group saw its own future in an alliance with Japan and had agreed to Japan's position in Shandong.

When the United States betrayed the Chinese cause, the students of Beijing University planned a public demonstration to protest this further humiliation in the face of Japanese aggression. The date chosen, May 7, was the anniversary of the infamous Twenty-one Demands, but as word came that the demonstration would be prevented by government forces, the date was moved up to May 4.

On the afternoon of May 4, three thousand students gathered peacefully in front of the southern gate of the Imperial City, known as Tiananmen ("Gate of the Heavenly Peace"), carrying slogan-covered banners exhorting Yuan Shikai to refuse to sign the peace treaty, calling for a China belonging to the Chinese, and denouncing as traitors those Chinese who were in favor of acceding to the Japanese demands. The students, some of whom were as young as fourteen, then marched to the American legation, where the top American official was absent and therefore unable to respond to the marchers. Frustrated by this, they went after the leaders of the Japanophile Anhui clique, burning down the home of one and beating up another. At this point, the police arrested thirty-two students.

What seemed like a youthful experiment in political action became a *cause célèbre* all over China. The cry went up from merchants in Shanghai to warlords from all over to free the students. More students prepared for a general strike and a boycott of Japanese goods and were in turn arrested. The merchants, followed by factory and railway workers, carried out the strike and paralyzed the country; finally the government in Beijing released all the students.

The unheard of had happened. The younger generation had led the older generations forward to champion a new and proud Chinese nationalism. A first step, one of many long and painful ones, had been taken toward a China once again owned and governed by the Chinese.

In retrospect, May 4, 1919, was to become a significant date in the history of the People's Republic of China. It marks the watershed between the first two decades of revolution fostered by Sun Yat-sen, which looked outside China's boundaries for ideals and inspiration, and the next three decades of turmoil within those boundaries, which led to a revolution based on Chinese ideas and programs. However, on this occasion, it was certainly not obvious to anyone that a young man who was an assistant librarian at the University of Beijing would, in another thirty years, take the center stage of Chinese politics.

13

MAO ZEDONG AND THE PEOPLE'S REPUBLIC

Mao Zedong [Mao Tse-tung] was born on December 26, 1893, in the rural village of Shaoshan in Hunan province. His family was part of a large clan, and his father was a successful, stingy, authoritarian peasant who rose to a position of relative wealth in his farming community. Mao was the oldest of three sons, and as such was expected by his father to help keep the family accounts as soon as he could read and use the abacus. Mao had more interest in reading legends and stories about the heroes of Chinese history, such as *Romance of the Three Kingdoms* and *Journey to the West*. His mother, like Chiang Kai-shek's, was a devout Buddhist, but there the resemblance ends, for Mao's mother was a warm, compassionate woman who sided with Mao in his wish to put schooling before working for his father. She even helped Mao save and borrow money to pay for school.

When the revolution broke out in 1911, Mao quit school to join the army but soon left and spent his pay on books. He applied to more schools and was accepted to one of the most progressive in China, the First Teachers' Training School in Changsha. Here he was fortunate enough to have an extraordinary teacher, a Pro-

Figure 57. Mao, on white pony, accompanies troops in Shaanxi province during the civil war against Guomindang forces, 1947. New China Pictures Co.

fessor Yang, trained as a philosopher in Edinburgh. Mao spent many hours in this man's classroom and home discussing the future of China with his professor and with other young people who were as bright and dedicated as he was.

In 1915, at age twenty-two, Mao published his first article in *New Youth*, titled "A Study of Physical Culture," and signed it "Mr. Twenty-eight Strokes," referring to the twenty-eight strokes required to make the characters of his name. He organized a student union and led protests against Japan's Twenty-one Demands.

A close friend of Mao's at this time recalled that Mao, who never brushed his teeth, took a bath, or tidied his room, berated his friend, a model of cleanliness, for wasting time on trivia when he should be thinking of cleaning up the world. Together with this same friend, Mao took an unusual summer trip in 1917. The two walked for six weeks through the countryside, where they met and talked with peasants. Mao recalled years later that the peasants had been warm and hospitable, always ready to offer food and shelter to the two students.

In 1918 Mao graduated from the First Teachers' Training School about the time his mother died of tuberculosis. It was a year of personal, professional, and geographic changes. Mao accepted the invitation of Professor Yang, now teaching at Beijing University, to come to Beijing; there Professor Yang found him a job as assistant librarian. When the Beijing University students marched on May 4, 1919, Mao was not in the capital but on a prolonged trip to Shanghai, where he saw off some of his friends who were leaving to study in France. Mao had been invited to join them but declined; his reason was that he preferred to learn more about his own country than to travel abroad.

When he returned to Beijing, Professor Yang had died, and Mao, who had fallen in love with his daughter, Yang Kaihui, married her. In most accounts of Mao's life, she is considered his first wife; he had been married by arrangement at fourteen, but that marriage, never consummated, was annulled.

From 1916 to 1927, there was no central government in China. Military contests between warlords passed control of Beijing back and forth between them in North China while Sun Yat-sen tried to establish a Guomindang (GMD) government in Guangzhou and parts of South China. The Bolsheviks had come to power in Russia in 1917, and after the events of May 1919, they saw China as fertile ground for their Marxist doctrines. Members of the Comintern, whose principal concern was international Communism, came to China in the early twenties and helped to start a Chinese Communist party in Shanghai. Chen Duxiu was a founding member. The Russian delegates, having tried unsuccessfully to work with the northern warlords, sought out Sun Yat-sen in Guangzhou, and Sun, whose previous support from Europe, the United States, and Japan had soured after 1919, welcomed the association with Lenin's government. His protégé, Chiang Kai-shek, now director of the newly established Huangpu (Whampoa) Military Academy near Guangzhou, was building a military force for the nationalist regime. The Comintern delegates decided that their interests lay in a Chinese Communist party aligned with, and even subordinate to, the Guomindang party. As long as Dr. Sun lived, the two parties cooperated, with the Guomindang dominant. Then Sun Yat-sen, working to the last for his vision of a Chinese republic, died of cancer in 1925.

Chiang Kai-shek, backed by troops trained at the Huangpu Military Academy, carried off a coup that made him Sun Yat-sen's successor, head of the Guomindang. He also married Dr. Sun's sister-in-law, Soong Mei-ling, which gave him access to financial backing. By 1927 Chiang had moved the center of operations of his military dictatorship, euphemistically called the Republic of China, from Guangzhou to Nanjing. Along the way, he had not only defeated warlords, he had also moved to eliminate his principal political opposition, the Chinese Communist Party (CCP). With the help of his friends in Shanghai, the Green Gang, he had authorized a massacre of members of the Communist labor union, and now, from Nanjing, he began a campaign to wipe out the CCP in China altogether.

Mao Zedong had joined both the Chinese Communist Party and the Guomindang in the early twenties, rising quickly to become a member of the Central Committee of the one and a director of propaganda for the other. But in 1925, he found himself at odds with both groups and left Shanghai, where he had been working for them, to go back to his native village in Hunan. There he organized the peasants into a local branch of the Communist Party, set up night schools for them modeled after traditional Chinese schools, and started peasant unions to fight against exploitive landlords. This movement spread rapidly throughout Hunan province, much to the alarm of both Chiang Kai-shek and the leaders of the Chinese Communist Party, who put the cause of the industrial urban worker before that of the peasant. When the Soviet-allied Chinese Marxists said "Workers Unite!" Mao said "Peasants Unite!" For Mao, China's revolution must not only better the peasant's lot, it must be founded on the peasant's lot. He saw the peasant, not the urban worker, as the "people" of Dr. Sun's Three People's Principles and the "proletariat" of Marxist theory.

When Chiang Kai-shek's determination to eliminate the Communist Party led to further brutal massacres, Mao forgot his differences with the Communists. The Guomindang in Hunan captured him in 1927, but he escaped by bolting into the underbrush two hundred yards from the execution site to which he was being led. Then, like the founder of the Han dynasty more than two thousand years before, he disappeared into the mountains, in this case on the Hunan-Jiangxi border. There he mustered a thousand followers among peasants and bandits and made them into an army, teaching them to read and write, training them in Marxist ideas, guerrilla tactics, and perhaps most important, insisting that they respect and help their fellow peasants, both men and women, rather than follow the raid-and-rape routine of the warlord armies.

The Long March

1934–35

From 1928 to 1934, Mao and other leaders of the Communist Party organized areas in Hunan and Jiangxi provinces into CCP enclaves which they called soviets and which were defended by troops they called the Red Army. (This echoed not only the Red Russians but also the Red Eyebrows of the first century A.D. and the Red Scarves of the fourteenth.) However, Chiang Kai-shek's campaign to kill off all Communists, planned with the help of German military advisors, was both relentless and increasingly successful. Among his victims was Mao's wife, who was arrested in Changsha in 1930 and, after refusing to renounce Communism, executed. By the fall of 1934, the leaders of the CCP had to choose between annihilation and flight to some place beyond the reach of the Guomindang. On October 16, 1934, the Red Army, with a core of about 50,000 soldiers, together with many noncombatant followers—men, women, and children, totalling over 100,000 (some estimates say as many as 300,000)—set out from Ruijin [Juichin], in eastern Jiangxi. They marched west and eventually north, on foot, pursued by Chiang's army, over roaring rivers, rugged mountain ranges, barren

Routes of the Long March, 1934–35

Figure 58. These soldiers of the People's Republic of China follow the trail taken through the snow-covered mountains in western Sichuan in 1934 by participants in the Long March. New China Pictures Co.

deserts, and treacherous swamps, until, a year and six thousand miles later—comparable to crossing the United States twice on foot—they reached Yan'an [Yen-an] ("Long Time Peace") in Shaanxi [Shen-hsi] province, finally out of Chiang Kai-shek's range. Of those that set out, only about twenty thousand reached Yan'an. The rest had been killed in battles with the Guomindang or died of exposure. Only one non-Chinese made the whole march, a German Communist whose job was to keep Stalin informed of and involved in the CCP strategies. About a quarter of the way along the route, radio contact with the outside world was lost, and in January of 1935, at a crucial meeting to plan the marchers' strategy, the power shifted from the hands of the Moscow-oriented German and his allies in the CCP to Mao. From this point on, Mao Zedong was the leader of the Chinese Communist Party, taking orders from no one, least of all Stalin. It was at this meeting that Mao received the support of a man who was to remain his closest colleague over the next four decades, his tireless and upright minister, Zhou Enlai [Chou En-lai].

From 1935 to 1945, in Yan'an, Mao and his followers set up their organization while living in rural simplicity in caves cut into the loess hillsides. The energy and spirit of this period is vividly captured in Edgar Snow's *Red Star over China*. In fact, it was this book that brought Mao and the CCP into the international spotlight, just as the *Globe* had introduced Sun Yat-sen to the world in 1896. In Yan'an, Mao adapted Marxist-Leninist ideas to the Chinese situation. The result was Mao Zedong Thought (later called Maoism and collected in *The Little Red Book*), a doctrine taught to tens of thousands of young people who came through Yan'an for training during this time. Mao Zedong Thought underlined the importance of the rural peasant as the foundation of Chinese Communist society.

World War II

Once again, the rattling of Japanese swords menaced, and Europe and Asia were swept into World War II. Our very abbreviated account of this devastating global engagement will focus on the consequences for China.

Japanese aggression escalated in 1930, when the Japanese took Manchuria, renamed it Manchukuo, and put the last Qing emperor on a puppet throne. By 1935 Japanese dominance had moved south of the Great Wall and threatened North China. On July 7, 1937, the Japanese crossed the Marco Polo Bridge, ten miles southwest of Beijing, to claim a strategic railway junction. (This bridge is a replica of the one visited by Marco Polo in 1290 and associated ever since with his description of the myriad lions carved in the marble balustrades of the original.) The Chinese armed opposition to this move, which was suppressed, gave Japan an excuse to occupy Beijing. Within a month, she had also captured Shanghai.

Caught in between, Chiang Kai-shek's armies fought for a year and then, in 1938, retreated up the Yangtse to Chongqing [Chung-

ch'ing] (Chungking), in Sichuan province. This became the Guomindang headquarters until the end of World War II. (Today this
city is the point of departure for cruises down the Yangtse.) Japan,
meanwhile, set up two more puppet governments, one in Beijing
and one in Nanjing.

Germany's move into Belgium in August of 1939 precipitated
the war in Europe. When the Japanese invaded Pearl Harbor on
December 7, 1941, the United States, neutral up to this point,
became one of the Allied forces, united against Japan and Germany. America's war with Japan, while predominantly carried out
through direct confrontation in the Pacific, also involved an alliance with the Guomindang forces in Chongqing. United States Air
Force pilots, the Flying Tigers led by General C. L. Chennault,
fought off Japanese bombers raiding Guomindang territory. When
the Japanese captured Burma and cut a crucial supply route, the
Burma Road, which came from railroad depots in India through
the mountains of northern Burma to Chongqing, President Roosevelt sent General Joseph ("Vinegar Joe") Stilwell to act as Chiang
Kai-shek's chief-of-staff, in charge of the airlift over the "hump"
of these same mountains.

These and other American personnel in Chongqing at the time
inevitably found themselves caught in the middle of the dispute
between the Guomindang and the Communists. Ultimately the
United States government remained faithful to Chiang Kai-shek.
Mao Zedong, from his headquarters in Yan'an, spent the war years
implementing peasant reforms in areas within the Japanese-oc-
cupied territories and encouraging a coordinated underground nationalism in a populace desperate for freedom from foreign oppression.
He offered to unite with the Guomindang in a common effort to
resist the Japanese. Chiang Kai-shek stubbornly refused any such
alliance; he put up a public front of fighting the Japanese with
American armaments, but in reality he was saving large quantities
of these armaments for use against the Communists when the war
was over.

When the Japanese surrendered, on August 14, 1945 (V-J
Day), civil war broke out between the Guomindang and the People's
Liberation Army (the Red Army). The Guomindang started with

three million troops armed with American equipment, while the Communists had a million soldiers, with not much equipment but a lot of discipline and spirit. The peasants who had been supported by Mao behind Japanese lines rallied to his side and sabotaged the Guomindang, bringing more and more American equipment into Communist hands with each successful action. In 1948 Chiang began to withdraw his followers, and a vast hoard of art treasures, to Taiwan. On October 1, 1949, the People's Republic of China was proclaimed in Beijing under Mao's leadership. The general-issimo, with American backing, established his Republic of China on Taiwan. Until his death in 1975, he nursed the futile hope that someday he would reclaim the Chinese mainland.

The People's Republic of China

For the first time ever in China's long and complicated history, the Middle Kingdom, All That Is under Heaven, was now a Chinese nation under nondynastic Chinese rule. But what in fact had changed? As Mao's biographer, Ross Terrill, has put it, Mao changed the "who" of Chinese society but not the "how." When the dust settled and the People's Republic got underway, the government was still as centralized as it had ever been, but the people who were important were not the educated scholars or the rich landowners but the members of the Communist Party, who were largely peasants. Confucian doctrine was thrown out, and Mao Zedong Thought was brought in. Here are two samples from *Quotations from Chairman Mao Zedong*—more familiarly known as *The Little Red Book*.

Our duty is to hold ourselves responsible to the people. Every word, every act and every policy must conform to the people's interests, and if mistakes occur, they must be corrected—that is what being responsible to the people means.[1]

1. From a speech made by Mao Zedong on August 13, 1945, as quoted in *Quotations from Chairman Mao Tsetung* (Beijing: Foreign Languages Press, 1972), 173.

> Without the efforts of the Chinese Communist Party, without the Chinese Communists as the mainstay of the Chinese people, China can never achieve independence and liberation, or industrialization and the modernization of her agriculture.[2]

During the early fifties, morale was high despite the enormous task the Chinese faced of rebuilding a new China on the rubble of a country that had not known stability or peace since the Taiping Rebellion. Mao, with Zhou Enlai as his prime minister, set up a "people's democratic dictatorship" to include all those who were not "enemies of the people." There was room for considerable latitude in interpreting this term.

The largest group of offenders were the landlords, who were subjected to everything from humiliation and reeducation to execution while their lands were redistributed among the peasants, at first on an individual basis and then under a centralized system of cooperatives.

While landlords were brought to heel, women were granted long-overdue equal rights with respect to marriage, divorce, and the ownership of property in the Marriage Law of 1950. Mao's inscription, in 1949, for the first issue of a magazine called *Women of New China* reads:

> Unite and take part in production and political activity to improve the economic and political status of women.[3]

Mao could direct his people in land management and social changes, but without outside help, he himself could not provide badly needed industrial aid and equipment. For this he turned to the Soviet Union under Stalin.

It will come as a surprise to most Americans that Stalin had backed Chiang Kai-shek during and after World War II, had urged Mao and the CCP to accept a coalition with him rather than fight a civil war and, right up to 1949, had tried to work out some

2. Ibid., 2.
3. Ibid., 296.

territorial deal with the generalissimo for a piece of China. Chiang could be manipulated, but Mao was defiantly his own man. Thus we can imagine the mixed feelings with which Mao, in late 1949, went to Moscow to work out a treaty for Russian aid, in the form of loans, and for mutual defense. As a result of the treaty, Russians trained Chinese to run industrial projects, develop mining areas, and rebuild urban centers while supplying them with military and industrial equipment, all of which the Chinese paid for with raw materials and produce. Travelers to the People's Republic today are aware of some of the results of Russian aid when they stay in the huge, unimaginatively designed tourist hotels built from Russian blueprints.

From the American point of view, by far the most significant result of this treaty was the Chinese involvement in the Korean War in 1950. Harrison Salisbury points to growing evidence that the war was instigated by Stalin, who wished to prevent Mao and President Truman from establishing formal diplomatic ties; the real causes of the Korean War are still in dispute, but the result was that Americans fought Chinese for the better part of two years. Throughout the fifties and sixties, the United States allied itself with Chiang Kai-shek's regime in Taiwan and shunned the People's Republic of China. Not until President Nixon's visit in 1973 was the way opened for a normalization of diplomatic relations between Beijing and Washington.

In 1959–60, after a decade of dedicated work to build a new China, terrible droughts led to widespread famine in 1961, and the program to develop small industry, known as the Great Leap Forward, failed to produce the anticipated results. After Stalin's death, the Beijing-Moscow alliance faltered. The people's energy for reconstruction was flagging, and the question at the top was how to rekindle it. There were two views. Mao, still convinced that a motivated rural populace was the only foundation for Chinese society, at first gave way to his challengers, who believed there would be strength and stability in a strong party bureaucracy and well-trained urban experts.

But then, afraid of losing control altogether, an aging Mao, encouraged by his third wife, Jiang Qing [Chiang Ch'ing], the ex-actress whom he had married in 1939, unleashed the Cultural

Revolution in 1966. (Mao's second wife, whom he married in 1930 after the death of his first, was the daughter of a Kiangxi landlord. She went with him to Yan'an, where they were divorced in 1937.) Mao decided that the new generation of Chinese youth needed the experience of revolution, so he turned to high-school-and-college-age young men and women who were not party members and designated them the Red Guards. Their assignment was to weed out "reactionaries." In effect, Mao and those who backed him in this move gave these young people license to overturn all social conventions. All persons of authority, in and out of the party, became the target of an adolescent fury. Parents were mocked, and teachers, professionals, and everyone else with any intellectual status or expertise were either sent to the countryside to work with their hands in the fields or they were jailed and, in many cases, tortured to death. Possibly a hundred million Chinese died or were sent to hard-labor camps, while countless more suffered total disruption of their lives, families, and careers.

All emblems of traditional culture, such as works of art, monuments, and buildings, were destroyed or defaced. The great book burning of Qin Shihuangdi in the third century B.C. was reenacted when the Red Guards tore up personal and public libraries and insisted that everyone read only Mao's *Little Red Book*. The official Cultural Revolution lasted from 1966 to 1969, but in fact the destruction of lives, of the social fabric of the country, and of personal and public property continued until Mao's death in 1976, and it has only recently been possible for the Chinese to speak openly of the terrible suffering during this anarchic period.

Mao Zedong died at the age of eighty-two in September 1976. In the last years of his life, his long association with Zhou Enlai, who died shortly before him, was marred when Zhou denounced the Cultural Revolution, while Mao, siding with his wife, defended it. With Zhou gone, the inevitable struggle over Mao's successor went on behind the scenes between Jiang Qing and her opponents. Jiang Qing, who, like a shade of the empress dowager Cixi, had hoped to succeed Mao herself, lost out when she and her three closest colleagues were arrested. The Gang of Four, as they were called, were held responsible for the crimes and devastation of the Cultural Revolution. They were tried and sentenced to life

Figure 59. Zhou Enlai, holding bouquet, returning to China after a trip to Cairo, in July 1965. To his right is Deng Xiaoping, the man who eventually succeeded Mao as leader of the People's Republic of China. New China Pictures Co.

imprisonment. The man who eventually rose, in 1979, to become the leader of the People's Republic of China was Deng Xiaoping [Teng Hsiao-p'ing], a veteran of the Long March and of the vicissitudes of Mao's government. In a long career, he had been in and out of favor with Mao, but now he came into his own with, as we are seeing, a new vision of China's future.

Deng, now in his eighties, has called for an adaptation of Maoist thought to the realities of China's needs. He is doing for Mao what Mao did for Marx in the 1940s. A sample of this is the editorial that appeared in the Communist Party newspaper, the *People's Daily*, on December 9, 1984:

One of the greatest contributions of Mao Zedong was the combination of theory and reality. Under the guidance of

155

this glorious thought, China won its revolutionary victory. . . . Party history tells us the combination of theory
and reality is the magic weapon. . . . So our slogan is:
Theory must be combined with reality.

Where does the reality of the 1980s point to for China? Deng
Xiaoping's view was published in the Chinese press on January
1, 1985. The following excerpt gives us an idea of his program
for China's future:

No country can now develop by closing its door. . . . We
suffered from this, and our forefathers suffered from
this. . . . Isolation landed China in poverty, backwardness,
and ignorance. . . . I am afraid that some of our old com-
rades have this fear, that after a generation of socialism and
Communism, it is unacceptable to sprout some capital-
ism. . . . It cannot harm us, it cannot harm us.

APPENDIX I

CHINA'S GEOGRAPHY

For the better part of its long history, China has been a self-contained world, a continent, as it were, unto itself, the center of gravity for Oriental civilization. Its culture has spread outward to Japan, Korea, and Southeast Asia, but very little has spread inward from these or other lands. The big exception was the spiritual invasion of Buddhism, which, ironically, came from India across the only border never extensively penetrated in either direction by an army, and which did much more to change Chinese life than either the Mongolian or the Manchu armed conquests of China.

Whether the empire was extensive, the size of today's People's Republic of China or even larger, or reduced to the territory of South China, the Chinese saw their world as the Middle Kingdom, "Zhongguo." The word *zhong*, meaning "middle," is used also in the term *zhong wen*, "middle language," i.e. Chinese.

Geography is responsible for this centripetalism and has determined China's relations with her neighbors, whether friend or foe. Look at a contour map of China and you will see how inevitable this should be. To the west and southwest, an arm of rugged highlands, made up of nine great mountain ranges, including the Himalayas, stretches from Southeast Asia to the western reaches

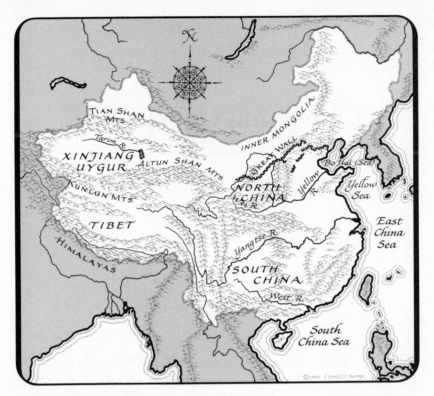

China's Topography

of Tibet. This massive barrier separates China from Southeast Asia, the Indian subcontinent, and Central Asia. In the northwest, locked between these ranges and the Tian Shan [T'ien Shan] range ("Heaven Mountains"), is the oval depression of the Tarim River basin. This was the east-west passage for the great trade routes that brought Chinese silk to Rome and Constantinople, and seeds, nuts, and other Eurasian exotica, to say nothing of artistic and religious influences, to China during the Han and Tang dynasties. Whenever Central Asian affairs became too disorderly, this trade ceased, the passage being closed by arms, and China withdrew from contact with the West.

China has always been most vulnerable along her northern boundary, where lesser mountain ranges border great open sweeps of grassy plain. Nomadic tribes, from time immemorial, descended from those plains onto the Chinese settlements and pillaged them for grain, livestock, and women. China's solution to this recurring scourge was the construction of a series of defenses, culminating in the present Great Wall, which ran at times almost two thousand miles from the Pacific coast to the Yumen, or Jade Gate, a point southeast of the Tian Shan range. As we have seen in chapter 4, these walls were effective for long periods of time. Only two great nomadic groups, the Mongols in the thirteenth century and the Manchu in the seventeenth, were ultimately able not only to push across the wall but to conquer all the rest of China as well. Even so, despite these two periods of foreign domination, the latter of which lasted longer than the whole two-hundred-year span of United States history, the Chinese regained control of their dominions and reestablished their national integrity. No wait has proved too long for them.

All along its eastern edge, China is water-bound, and except for minor incursions by Japanese pirates in the fifteenth century and European traders from the sixteenth on, this coast remained virtually unthreatened until the last century, when the Europeans pushed inland up rivers and established an imperialist presence. The Japanese made an attempt at conquest during World War II, but their efforts lasted for less than a decade, and they never penetrated far back from the coast.

Geography, if nothing else, is the reason why China today is the only nation in the world to have preserved its political and cultural integrity for more than three thousand years. Internal geography has also been responsible for this cohesion. First of all, the boundaries just described were as forbidding from the inside as they were from the outside. Expansion beyond them was difficult. Secondly, most of China is mountainous, and life in mountains or valleys is conducive to insularity. There is a popular legend about a village so remote that when travelers come upon it, they witness the dress and customs of a bygone era. By the same token, uprisings such as the Taiping Rebellion or the Communist insurgency were able to swell unchecked to enormous proportions since members of "secret societies" or forbidden political parties could hide in mountain pockets.

It is easiest to divide China into three major parts: North China, South China, and the peripheral, outer China.

North China's most important feature is the Yellow River, which begins in Tibetan highlands as a narrow, eastward-flowing stream, then makes a big inverted U north into Inner Mongolia and back down into China proper. Before it turns east again to the Pacific, it is met by the river of classical China, the Wei. The Yellow River is twenty-seven hundred miles long, and for much of its eastern length, as it cuts into a plateau of loamy yellow soil built up by dust blown down for eons from the Mongolian grasslands, it is quite literally yellow in color. *Loess* is the term used to describe such windblown deposits, whether in North China or along the Mississippi.

This combination of a great water source and rich soil ought to be perfect for establishing an agricultural society, and indeed it was just this that attracted Neolithic cultures to this area. However, the Yellow River is often called "China's sorrow" because it alternately floods and dries up, changes its course without warning, its unexpected deluges killing thousands, and is so silted that transportation along its half-mile-wide lower course is impossible except with shallow, raftlike craft. The vagaries of the Yellow River are responsible for the high degree of centralization that has been characteristic of Chinese government from the time of the legendary Yu to the present. Highly coordinated social organization was essential for controlling the river, and as explained in Chapter 1, law and order and ultimately survival depended on a leader's making this his first priority.

All of classical China's great capital cities were built close to the conjunction of the Wei and Yellow rivers. Until the Song dynasty in the tenth century, this was China's heartland. With the rise of the Southern Song dynasty in the twelfth century, South China became equally important.

South China begins just north of the Yangtse River and includes the Sichuan basin, the mountains to the west of that, and everything to the south. Once again, the most important feature is a river, but this time it is a river that is navigable by steamer along the lower half of its thirty-three-hundred-mile length. The Yangtse is one of China's major transportation routes and a vital artery for South China especially, because the predominance of mountainous terrain in this area makes road and train travel, let alone travel by bicycle, horse, or foot, arduous. The scenery along its banks has inspired artists and poets over the centuries; its fabled gorges are still a favorite for today's travelers. The lower half of the Yangtse basin has been China's "rice bowl" ever since the sixth century, when the Sui emperors built the Grand Canal to bring agricultural produce from South China to their capital in Chang'an.

Perhaps the most famous of South China's landscapes is in the environs of Guilin, in Guangxi province. Here strange mountains, shaped like upended loaves of French bread, rise from the banks of the Li River. We know this scenery from the scroll paintings of Chinese masters. But anyone who travels down the Li realizes that these artists were not visionaries—the shapes are nature's own.

The division between north and south has frequently been political as well as physical, for instance during the Northern and Southern dynasties, the Northern and Southern Song dynasties, and even as recently as the warlord period after World War I. Furthermore, the Three Kingdoms of the fourth century (see chapter 6) coincided with geographical regions. The Wei kingdom was North China, the Shu was Sichuan province, and the Wu was the rest of South China.

Finally we come to the outer regions of today's China: Tibet, Xinjiang Uygur, and Inner Mongolia. They are the areas inhabited in the past by the tribes that were considered barbarians. Today these peoples are referred to as "national minorities." Tibet (called Xizang [Hsi-tsang], or Western Treasure-house, by the Chinese today) was an autonomous political area throughout most of history, difficult to reach or to govern from the outside. It is kept remote by the Chinese, who, for reasons that are not clear, allow visitors to travel there only in tours, and even then, special visas are required. Xinjiang Uygur (often spelled Sinkiang Uighur), home of the Moslem Uygur people, includes the Tarim River basin. It was in this area that the great Han governor-general of the Western Territories, Ban Chao, made his name in the second century A.D. Today, because of its proximity to the Soviet Union, it is a militarized area with only two or three cities open to visitors. Mongolia's history is full of nomadic tribes who not only raided traditional

China's world but also, under Attila in the fourth century, invaded the declining Roman Empire. Today Mongolian tribes still live a nomadic life in tents, or yurts, much as they must have for thousands of years, but inside them the twentieth century is represented by the department-store bureaus, which contain traditional tribal costumes.

In today's atlas, China is vast—the third largest country in the world after the Soviet Union and Canada. But so much of its terrain is inhospitable mountains or barren windswept plains that its present population of over a billion people must live and find subsistence on less than a third of its territory. Sichuan province, where water is abundant, the terrain relatively flat, and the climate temperate, leads in population density, followed by the eastern areas of North China along the Yellow River and the plains north of Beijing, the entire eastern coastline, and the Yangtse River area.

This uneven geography makes population control a first priority, a major determinant of China's success in her urgent push to modernize. How can all these people be fed? What are the effects of pollution on agricultural production? Can barren hillsides be reforested? Is life possible in a desert? China's solutions to these and related problems will set the standards for the rest of the world. Whatever China's isolation in the past, she is now part of a world community, and we all share in her predicament—and her promise.

APPENDIX II

HIGHLIGHTS OF CHINESE ART

To the Western eye, Chinese art is at once appealing and foreign. The delicacy of a misty black-and-white landscape casts a spell we don't quite fathom; the massive presence of a bronze cauldron commands our attention, but we may wonder why. The following section points to some of the links between Chinese art, history, and culture—links that may help to explain our intuitive responses and make possible a better understanding of the many masterpieces of Chinese art to be seen on display all over the world.

Prehistoric Art

c 5000–2000 B.C.

Pottery samples, the ubiquitous gauge of prehistoric craftsmanship, help to identify sites of the Neolithic Yangshao culture that grew up along the Yellow River basin between the fifth and third millennia B.C. One of the most-visited sites of this culture is at Banpo [Pan-p'o], an excavated village located six miles east of present-day Xi'an. In the adjacent museum are Stone Age artifacts that include polished pots, stone ax blades, nets, and bone needles. Most interesting are the pots because they are painted with designs that give us clues to the imaginative life of their makers.

The pots were formed by hand from clay coils into a variety of bowl and jar shapes which were then painted and fired. One of the most prevalent designs is the fish motif. At first the fish figures are quite realistic, but gradually they evolve into schematic, geometrical patterns, with two or more fish coming nose to nose in a meeting of triangles punctuated with an eye each, or meshing into a gridded diamond with tails on the four corners.

These Neolithic fish designs are like the initial statement of a theme at the beginning of a set of variations; fish and dragons, a later incarnation of fish, will appear again and again in Chinese art, symbols of the crucial role that water and waterborne creatures play. The Banpo fish are simply designs to us now; we do not know what they meant to their makers, but we can guess a little when we recall the story of the first legendary emperor, Fuxi. One of his great contributions was teaching his people to fish with nets. Another was the recording of the mystical diagrams from the back of the "dragon-horse" that rose before him from the river. Fuxi and his consort, Nuwa, were described as having human torsos and dragon tails, but the dragon tails typically depicted in Eastern Han relief carvings of the second century A.D. are certainly fish tails. (See figure 1.)

Around 3500 B.C., a new sort of pottery, commonly referred to as Black Pottery, replaces the Painted Pottery of the Yangshao culture and is associated with the prehistoric culture known as Longshan. While the Black Pottery includes gray and white pots, the eggshell-thin black pots are distinctive of Longshan pottery and perhaps wrongly often considered as representative of all Longshan pottery. They were wheel-thrown and made of a ferrous clay that turned black from the high temperatures and the smoke inside sealed kilns.

While surface design reveals the artistic imagination of the Yangshao culture, shape was the primary concern of the Longshan artist. Whether tall beakers with wide flaring rims or tripod cooking vessels with pitcher necks, the shapes both express the potter's joy in form and presage the shapes that were to emerge in the next artistic medium, bronze. The shapes were also practical: An udder-shaped tripod pitcher with hollow legs stood in a fire, and the liquid inside the legs was more efficiently heated than it would have been in a large round pot.

It is important to stop here for a moment, before moving into the great Bronze Age of the Shang dynasty, and note that the transition from Stone Age (pottery and stone artifacts) to Bronze Age (bronze is an alloy of copper and tin) in China continues to present scholars with great unanswered mysteries. The bronze artifacts look like and are made in ways similar to the preceding pottery ones, but they required metallurgic skills that seem to have appeared full blown from no known source either within or without the indigenous culture. In the West, there was a definite transition from copper work to sophisticated bronze techniques, during which both the hammer and the forge were used, but in China, the leap was made from pottery to bronze with very little evidence of the use of copper and no intermediary period in which the hammer was used in working bronze. How did it happen?

Shang and Zhou Dynasties

c 2000–221 B.C.

Whatever the answer to the mystery, the bronze artifacts of the Shang dynasty (1600–1100 B.C.) are, by any standards, awesome artistic and technological achievements. While it is easy to imagine a single potter of the earlier periods sitting down to handle the raw clay and ending up with a finished pot, it is hard to conceive of the teams of sophisticated miners, smelters, sculptors, and foundrymen who all had a hand in producing a bronze pot. Archeological evidence makes it clear that these bronzes were produced in the capital cities for the Shang court. This was not a folk art but an official, palace art produced for use by the monarch and his ministers as they carried out the affairs of state.

One of the more remarkable stages in the production of these works was the creation of the molds. In excavations of Shang sites, fragments of two kinds of molds have been found. The first is a clay original, or positive mold. More clay was pressed around this, removed (in pieces), and left to harden. This is a second, negative mold. Once the pieces of the negative mold were dried and hard, fine relief carvings were incised, in reverse, on their inner surfaces. Then the pieces were reassembled and bound together to form the receptacle for the molten bronze. The intricate linear designs that cover the surfaces of most of the Chinese bronzes of this era attest to the skill of the Shang craftsmen. The artist had to imagine what the finished design would look like and then, with a sure hand, carve it in reverse into clay in fluid, often barely separated, lines.

(Later, during the Zhou dynasty, the "lost wax" method, still used by today's bronze casters, was invented. Here, in its simplest version, an original form is made in wax, which is then surrounded by a clay mass with holes at the top; the whole mass is baked until the wax evaporates, and then the molten bronze is poured in. The bronze cools and hardens, the clay is cracked away, and the finished work is polished to eliminate imperfections. This is the only way to cast the pierced or undercut bronze works that first appear in the Zhou era.)

The Shang artist did not make up his designs as he went along. He was guided by a "hieratic" style, that is, a style in art determined by religious or ritual practices. In the case of the Shang, the bronze vessels appear to have been made for use in seasonal ceremonies involving animal sacrifices, offerings of agricultural products, and the brewing of grain wines. Large cauldrons, smaller three- or four-legged pots, both rectangular and rounded, long-necked three-legged pitchers, pitchers shaped like animals—all served a particular purpose. In some cases, the shapes clearly indicate a debt to earlier pottery forms, as in the three-legged containers, while in others, they tell us that animals, such as bulls, sheep, birds, and dragons, were key to the ceremonial occasions.

In the decoration of the surfaces, three motifs prevail throughout the artistic evolution of these bronzes. The first and most prominent is a mask characterized by large round protruding eyes, a long nose with low flaring nostrils, and curling ears that frame the sides. This mask is called taotie [t'ao-t'ieh], literally "glutton," but the

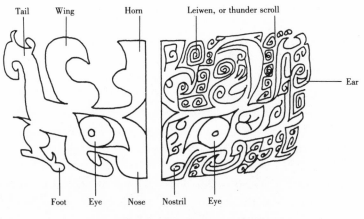

Tail   Wing   Horn   Leiwen, or thunder scroll

Ear

Foot   Eye   Nose   Nostril   Eye

Kui, or dragon   Half mask of taotie, or glutton

Figure 60. Line sketch, taken from photo of Shang bronze ting (see figure 9, page 16), showing taotie, or glutton mask, which can also be seen as two confronting kui, or dragons. Photograph courtesy of the Freer Gallery of Art, Smithsonian Institution, Washington, D.C.

name was first used in the third century B.C.; there is no record of what the Shang themselves called it.

If we take the designs on the ting in figure 9 (page 16) as an example of the taotie mask, we can see the other two motifs as components of the mask. Use the drawing in figure 60. Divide the mask in half at the vertical which is the nose. Each side represents a winged animal seen in profile: The eye of the taotie is still the eye of the animal, the nostril of the taotie is its nose, the form above the eye of the taotie is its wing, and the ear of the taotie is its tail. This creature is called the kui [k'uei] in third-century-B.C. writings and was later assumed to represent a single-footed dragon. In some earlier versions the kui has a long fish tail, once again connecting the dragon with fish and water. Two kui placed face to face make a mask; the overall effect is teasing and ambiguous.

The third motif can be seen in figure 9 in the spaces not occupied by the dragon or mask components. This is a spiral design, called the leiwen [lei-wen] ("thunder scroll"), which is used over and over to create texture in what would otherwise be blank areas. The dragon flies through mist and clouds on the Shang bronzes just as he will in a Song painting twenty-five hundred years later.

On the later Shang bronzes, the literal motifs of the taotie, the kui, and the leiwen evolve into abstracted components, often used separately. The wing of the dragon becomes a *G* motif, repeated alone without the rest of the body; the eyes of the mask become protruding dots on either side of a vertical line with nothing but the repeated thunder scroll to hold them in place; or the vertical nose line becomes the emphasized joint between two planes and is embellished with three-dimensional curlicues that have nothing to do with the original mask.

During the Eastern Zhou dynasty (770–221 B.C.), which was subdivided into the Spring and Autumn periods (770–476 B.C.) and the Warring States period (475–221 B.C.), bronze technology in the service of music became so sophisticated that the Marquis of Yi, ruler of the Warring State of Zeng, was buried with a set of sixty-five bronze bells. Excavated in 1978, the biggest is five feet high and the smallest only a few inches, and all are clapperless; they span more than five octaves in perfectly tuned tones. Each one makes two different tones, depending on where it is hit. In the West at this time, the biggest bronze bell known was only eight inches high.

The use of bronze in the arts of the first two millennia B.C. of Chinese history is so prevalent that it is easy to overlook other materials, but mention must be made of jade, which was used to make artistic and musical objects. Flat discs with perforated centers and relief designs representing celestial bodies were symbols of heaven, while rectangular columns with rounded hollow cores were symbols of earth. Small pieces of jade were used to seal the orifices of the dead in the belief that this would slow decay. Ceremonial jade axes, jade chimes, flat jade dragons with scrolling bodies and tails—all these objects testify to the high value placed on this mysteriously colored, cool, hard stone.

Jade and Dragons

Here it makes sense to interrupt the chronological sequence of this account with a few words about two things long favored by the Chinese but rather foreign to the Westerner: jade and dragons, i.e. Chinese dragons.

Jade has a long history in China as a stone considered more precious than any other gem or mineral, gold and silver included. It is associated with five virtues: charity, modesty, courage, justice, and wisdom. It is also associated with the five-colored stones made by Nuwa, the legendary consort of Fuxi, which she used to patch up the heavens. It is called the Stone of Heaven; the Chinese character for jade is the same as that for king but with a dot added; the most famous Chinese novel, *The Dream of the Red Chamber*, written in the eighteenth century, is about a hero called Precious Jade who was, in fact, a piece of jade incarnate. One could go on and on with such examples of the importance of jade. Instead, we will take note of some of the special physical qualities that justify its reputation.

First of all, jade comes in two forms: jadite and nephrite. The difference between them is chemical and hard to discern without either sophisticated equipment or a great deal of expertise. Most Chinese artifacts from ancient times to the present are of nephrite. Both stones are hard; rated on a scale of one to ten, nephrite rates about six and jadite about seven (quartz also rates seven, while diamonds rate ten). Jade cannot be carved but must be ground with abrasive powder by hand or with a wheel. The pure state of both forms is a milky white, often dubbed "mutton fat" for its resemblance to glossy animal fat, but chemical impurities provide a color range from deep to light green, beige, and gray. The very hardest and most perfect jade stones are exorbitantly priced, while lower-quality stones, invariably nephrite, are found in every trinket shop for next to nothing. It takes a very practiced eye to distinguish a high-quality jade, and as in the diamond trade, even the experts can be fooled.

The Chinese dragon is even more ubiquitous than jade, and it must be established immediately that this creature has absolutely nothing to do with the devourers of maidens or challengers of saints and heroes of European culture—nor is it associated with the underworld or the forces of evil. Rather, the Chinese dragon, which can assume many forms, is a symbol of water in its many manifestations: rivers, lakes, mists, and clouds (with their accompanying thunder and lightning, and rain). Chinese dragons live in the deepest reaches of rivers and caves and rise to hide in the

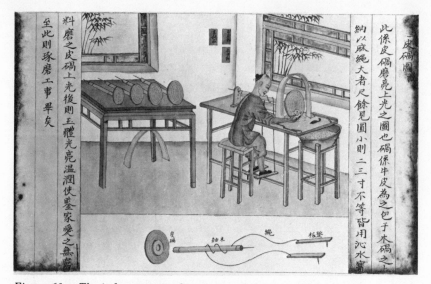

Figure 61. *The jade carver in this nineteenth-century print uses foot-powered drills for making openwork designs in the hard stone.* The Metropolitan Museum of Art, gift of Heber R. Bishop, 1902

mists and clouds of heaven. They can be moody, tempestuous, languorous, shy, terrifying, but never evil. They represent a powerful but ultimately beneficent force in the lives of men.

The visual representations of dragons evolved from something that looks like a large-headed eel into a creature with the fire-breathing head of a bull, the horns of an antelope, the legs and claws of a tiger, and the tail of a lizard. The dragon became the emblem of the ruler, whether king or emperor—the man who sat on the "dragon throne" and wore "dragon robes." As in the stories of the three virtuous rulers, the legendary Yao, Shun, and Yu, whose reputations rest on their success at flood control, these imperial dragon symbols signify the inseparable relation between political power and the role of water in human affairs.

Qin Dynasty

Moving on in our chronology, we come to the time of the unification of the Chinese empire under the Qin dynasty. The tomb of the great unifier, Qin Shihuangdi, is currently considered the single most remarkable artistic achievement of this period (221–207 B.C.). In fact, there is nothing like it in the whole world. Hundreds of thousands of workers labored for the burial arrangements of one man. The tantalizing description of the actual burial chamber inside the tumulus (see chapter 4) may be verified in the next decade as this is excavated. What has been excavated thus far, to the east of the tumulus, are the thousands of life-size clay warriors standing in battle formation, each one an individual, each one assembled from separately cast clay sections. In fact, this army is significant not only artistically but also politically, historically, and psychologically as a documentation of Shihuangdi's power, his conquering army, and his implacable megalomania.

This clay army has precedents in Shang and Zhou burial customs. The Shang buried real victims—stabbed or decapitated men and women—with the deceased. During the Zhou era, this practice stopped, and archeologists have found, in lieu of skeletons, small clay figurines. No examples from either era, however, begin to compare in scale with Qin Shihuangdi's army. The custom of burying clay armies with the emperor or other royal persons continued in the Han dynasty, but the figures uncovered in these later tombs are at most three-quarter-size, and the military presence is joined by that of entertaining dancers and musicians. No one else anywhere on earth has ever been buried with such single-minded attention to military protection in the afterworld.

Han Dynasty

The long-lived Han dynasty (206 B.C.–220 A.D.), which supplanted the Qin rule soon after Shihuangdi's burial, gave China her first great era of multifaceted national culture. The highly focused art used in the court rituals of the Shang and Zhou era gave way to a new sort of official art: the illustration of Confucian classics and of Sima Qian's *Records of the Historian*. The depictions of great legendary and historical personages and events emphasize the virtuous behavior of leaders, subjects, parents, and children. The stone walls of the Wu family tombs in Jiaxiang, Shandong province, covered with relief carvings, provide the most famous collection of such scenes. These have become widely known through rubbings, as in figures 1 (Fuxi and Nuwa) and 14 (attempt to assassinate Qin Shihuangdi).

Other examples of Han art give us a sampling of various activities throughout the empire: Reliefs on clay bricks depict the peasants harvesting rice, collecting salt, or hunting deer while wooden or clay statuettes represent acrobats, musicians, and dancers.

A Western Han tomb recently discovered at Mawangdui, on the eastern outskirts of Changsha, Hunan province, contained what is now the earliest known example of Chinese painting. In black ink and color pigment on silk, this is a two-meter-long banner, which was found covering an inner coffin. Robed human figures in the middle enact scenes from legend and ceremonies while around them snakelike dragons, realistic birds, and stylized plant forms represent the inhabitants of heaven and the underworld.

Paper was invented sometime during the Han period. According to tradition, it was first brought to the attention of the emperor (who was later deified as the god of papermakers) by a court eunuch in 105 A.D. Archeological finds of paper made from raw silk seem to predate this event. (In Europe, paper was not produced until the twelfth century, when it replaced parchment vellum as a writing surface.) One of Qin Shihuangdi's generals, obviously a cultured military man in the best Confucian tradition, is credited with the invention of the paintbrush (his was made of a bamboo stick and animal hairs) back around 220 B.C. Until then, writing had been done with bamboo pens. One line of characters was written vertically down single strips of bamboo, which were then bound together by cord as in a split-bamboo table mat. The vertical format of the written line was retained, but now several lines could be placed together on one scroll of paper. During the Han period, calligraphy with the brush on paper became a specialized art incorporating several different styles of script.

Bronze mirrors, jade artifacts, and lacquerware, all of which had been made ever since the Warring States period, complete the range of Han artistry and provide further evidence of the dynasty's sophisticated graphic techniques. Han artists were ac-

Figure 62. Western Han (206 B.C.–8 A.D.) wooden figurines of musicians were found in Mawangdui tomb, Changsha, Hunan province. New China Pictures Co.

Figure 63. Pottery figurines of acrobats are from a Western Han tomb in Jinan, Shandong province. New China Pictures Co.

Figure 64. This Han dynasty mirror was found in exceptional condition in recent excavations of a Han tomb. The designs on its back are thought to represent stars. Dong Ronggui, New China Pictures Co.

complished, they had a wealth of materials to work with, and their subject matter was drawn from legend, history, and folklore. Even when the stories they told served to reinforce the official Confucian doctrine, the expression is full, poetic, individual.

Buddhist Art

At the collapse of the Han empire in 220, China fell into a disunity that lasted until the reunification by the first Sui emperor in 589. During the period of decentralization, the rise of Buddhism provided the impetus for the most notable artistic achievements.

The three Buddhist cave shrines most visited today date from the fourth and fifth centuries. These are the Yungang [Yun-kang]

174

Caves of Datong, in Shanxi province, 167 miles west of Beijing, the Longmen Caves near Luoyang in Henan province, and the Mogao Grottoes near Dunhuang [Tun-huang] in western Gansu [Kansu] province. They all contain statues and wall paintings illustrating the life and varied manifestations of the Buddha. The draped figures in the earliest frescoes and statues reveal the influence of the Greco-Indian, or Gandharan, style, which was the legacy of Alexander the Great.

What is most remarkable about these early shrine sculptures is the figures' expressions of inward serenity and detachment. They convey, in a way that words cannot, the spiritual message of the Buddha, a message very different indeed from that of the earlier Han wall reliefs, which illustrated historical episodes with a Confucian moralizing flavor. Buddhist art is China's most spiritual art.

Buddhism also brought a new architecture to China, in the form of the pagoda, a tower temple evolved from its Indian version, the stupa—which, in turn, had grown out of the mound shrine covering the bones of the Buddha. The first Chinese pagoda on record is one built near Nanjing in the middle of the third century A.D., but it has not survived. The more recent examples that we see today have tapered towers composed of as many as fifteen stories, representing different levels of the Buddhist heaven, separated by overhanging, and often curled, roofs. These pagodas were built around interior staircases with exteriors that were round, square, or octagonal and built of brick, wood, or stone. They rose above the landscape like beacons pointing the way to heaven and, from the sixth to ninth centuries, lured increasing numbers of devotees away from the affairs of this world to life in the monastery.

Sui and Tang Dynasties

Sui Wendi, who reunified China at the end of the sixth century, and his son, the only other Sui ruler, were responsible for incredible monuments of architecture and engineering. The best known of their enterprises was the first Grand Canal, but they also built pagodas and bridges. However, the coercive measures taken to supply forced labor for this mammoth burst of state works fostered rebellion; the second Sui emperor was assassinated, and the Count of Tang took the throne.

The Tang dynastic era (618–907) is China's golden age of culture. Everything before seems to lead to the achievements of this era, and everything after looks back to them, maintaining, enhancing, or reacting against the great Tang standards.

The second emperor of the Tang, Taizong (r. 626–649), one of the most tolerant rulers of all times, set the tone for this era when he reestablished the great trade route across Central Asia and welcomed not only bearers of foreign art objects to his court but also the representatives of new foreign religions: Muslims, Nestorian Christians, Zoroastrians. The Tang capital of Chang'an (present-day Xi'an) became the foremost cosmopolitan center of its day under his reign and continued as such for over two hundred years. Because the art of this period shows the effects of exposure to foreign influences, the Tang style is often called the International Style of Chinese art.

The enthusiasm of Tang Taizong is expressed in the grand stone relief sculptures of his favorite horses. These were in his tomb, but some are now on display in the Shaanxi Provincial Museum in Xi'an and are well known throughout the world through rubbings. With unparalleled gusto, they gallop harnessed but riderless, with knotted manes and tails, across empty space.

The most widely known Tang art is also the most easily identified: the green, yellow, and blue glazed pottery statuettes of equestrians, horses, camels, dancers, musicians, and acrobats. These figures, produced in molds and then colored with an abandon unique in Chinese glazing styles, were probably as much used for export as for popular and funerary purposes. Like their less sophisticated Han counterparts, they tell us a great deal about the life and activities of their day.

The ornamentation of bronze hand mirrors is typical of the eclectic approach of the Tang International Style. Where the Warring States and Han mirrors were simple circles decorated on their backs with designs of either geometric celestial symbols or scenes of historical significance, the Tang mirrors have petal-shaped edges, and on their backs, lions, grapes, and flowers of Persian origin curl with a sensuality unknown in previous Chinese bronzes. These mirrors also testify to the great popularity of grape wine in Tang China. The story of the eighth-century poet Li Bai, in chapter 7, further reminds us that drunkenness could be almost a state of grace.

The categories of Tang art we have so far considered reflect techniques or styles unique to their times. However, there are two great cultural developments that originated in the middle of the Tang era and that have profoundly affected Chinese art and culture ever since. Printing by block is one, and landscape painting is the other. These are so significant that we will step out of the chronological sequence once again and devote a separate section to each.

Printing in China

Printing of both images and books in China developed out of two practices: the making of rubbings and the use of stone or clay seal stamps. The first was done to reproduce on paper the Confucian texts that had been carved into smooth stone surfaces, and the second was a Daoist practice for making magic signs, picked up by the Buddhists for reproducing, over and over, as an act of prayer, the image of the Buddha.

Silk was first used as a surface for holding ink markings but was largely replaced by paper after it was invented in about the first century. Black ink, known most accurately as *encre de Chine* in French and misleadingly as India ink in English, had been around since Shang times. We know that by the third century A.D., this was made by mixing soot, or lampblack, collected from a cover placed over wicks burning in oil, with either gum or gluten. The mixture was hardened into small blocks, which, when rubbed against a smoothly sloped stone wetted with water, became an indelible ink which collected in a bowl carved into the bottom of the sloped stone.

To make a rubbing, a piece of thin paper is affixed with rice paste to the surface of the engraved stone and then tamped all over on its outer side with a rounded, inked cloth pad, until all the areas in contact with uncarved stone are blackened and the carved areas are revealed in white. This is similar to putting a piece of paper over a penny and running a lead pencil back and forth over the paper until the image and letters on the coin show up. Image and letters are not reversed.

In the stamping of images with a seal stone, the image is carved in reverse, inked, and then stamped downward on a piece of paper, where it appears right side around.

Both of these practices were common by the time of Tang Taizong in the seventh century, and he himself had a library at Chang'an of at least fifty-four thousand scrolls that must have included many samples of both techniques. Under his patronage, two Chinese pilgrims went to India and returned to Chang'an with Buddhist texts. In the monastery that he built for them, part of which remains as the monument in Xi'an known as the Great Goose Pagoda, and in monasteries in other parts of China, the urgent desire to reproduce these translated texts in large quantities not only helped to spread Buddhism but led to the invention of block printing—which in turn led to book printing.

Sometime during the eighth century, the stone-rubbing and seal-stamp methods of reproduction were merged into a block-print technique initially used for making images; but by the ninth century, it was used for block printing as well. Block-printed books and images are still made today in China, and the method for the former, though it requires skill and time, is ingeniously straightforward.

First, two pages of text are written side by side with brush and ink on one thin piece of paper. A column between pages gives a folio number and the book title. This sheet is then placed face down, while the ink is still wet, on a wood block which has been coated with rice paste. The ink is absorbed into this paste, the paper is removed, and the reversed ink shapes of the characters are left on the block. The engraver then cuts away all the areas not inked; mistakes can be corrected by gluing in tiny pieces of wood. The engraved surface is brushed with ink, a clean paper is placed over it, and a wide, clean brush is passed back and forth over the back until the paper has received the full impression of the characters on its downward face. The printed paper is pulled away and allowed to dry. When all the pages of a text have been printed in sets of two in this manner, they are each folded, blank sides together, and sewn into a book down the back, or open, edges. The folded edges are left intact as they list the folio, chapter and/or title along the front of the book.

Chinese texts are printed in vertical columns that are read, top to bottom, in a sequence going from right to left. In a book, the first page is our last page. The tradition of using columns comes from the Zhou period custom of writing on strips of bamboo.

Movable-type printing, using characters made of clay, was invented in the eleventh century in China, four centuries before Gutenberg produced his famous Bible in Europe. However, because the Chinese system of writing required tens of thousands of movable characters, this method was not extensively used until the eighteenth century, when either copper or tin type was set. The earliest known Chinese block print dates from 770, and the first block-printed book from 868; since the earliest samples that have come down to us are highly developed samples, we can assume that there were earlier versions. The great patron of the arts Tang Xuanzong (r. 713–756) probably saw some of the first block prints ever made when he and his much loved lady, Yang Guifei, entertained at court in Chang'an.

In the tumultuous last century of Tang rule, the tradition of religious tolerance evaporated. Buddhist monasteries and convents became thorns in the sides of Tang Xuanzong's successors because they were now powerful institutions that attracted many young men and women who otherwise would have become soldiers, laborers, and bearers of children, much needed by the latter Tang emperors. In desperation, one of these rulers passed the infamous edict of 845 calling for the destruction of forty-six hundred Buddhist temples, and when this was carried out, countless precious editions of the first printed books were lost. Fortunately, even though the books, and soon the Tang empire itself, were lost forever, the invention lived on, and during the Song dynasty (960–1279) especially, book printing, predominantly done with block prints rather than movable type, flourished as never before. These Song editions form the foundation for most great collections of Chinese books today.

Calligraphy, Landscape Painting, and Poetry

We come now to the great hallowed trio of Chinese arts and letters: calligraphy, landscape painting, and poetry. From the height of the Tang period on, highest honors were accorded to those who excelled in these three pursuits. Invariably such persons were men who had learned these skills in the course of their studies for the several levels of the civil-service examinations. A young man who aspired to a high government position needed to prove his proficiency as a poet, painter, and calligrapher, and he learned at a young age to fuse the three.

It is hard for the Western mind to understand the role of calligraphy in this triumvirate. We tend to think of writing as a purely technical process because our letters are simply phonetic symbols, and only in rare instances in Western culture, such as in medieval illuminated manuscripts, have they been considered as aesthetic forms. Chinese characters, in contrast, are pictographs, and although they have been highly abstract, a long aesthetic tradition has shaped their evolution. There is a fixed order in which the strokes in any character must be made, just as there is a strict notion of the proper proportion and placement of each stroke in relation to the overall composition of the character. Each time a calligrapher begins a character, he must have the entire arrangement in his mind's eye and then produce it on paper in perfect balance. When the time comes to write a poem, the sentiment of the words must be reflected in the elegance of the calligraphy. Thus it can be imagined that writing out a beautifully balanced text of many columns of characters on a long scroll required decades of training.

Such training developed the vocabulary of brushstrokes essential for any painting made with brush on paper; the Chinese painter has always had two points of reference of equal importance by which to judge his finished work: the calligraphic appeal of his brushstrokes and his pictorial treatment of the subject matter, whether landscape, figure, flora, or fauna. It was only in the twentieth century that Western painters thought to consider the brushstroke as an artistic element in its own right, and as in the case of Franz Kline, the debt to Oriental calligraphy is openly acknowledged. In the drawings of Leonardo da Vinci, Michelangelo, Rembrandt, or Van Gogh, for example, the pen lines and brushstrokes may be seen as brilliant, but they are not thought of as being calligraphic—that is, derived from the art of writing.

But let's go back to the Tang era. We know that they had paper or silk as a painting surface, and they had black ink. Brushes had been in existence since the third century B.C. In paintings before and throughout most of the Tang era, the emphasis was on the figure: Murals on Buddhist shrines showed religious figures, paintings done at court showed historical figures or court society (figures 26, 65). These works consist of black ink outlines filled in with flat color planes. Landscape settings, if indicated at all, were reduced to single rocks or trees that appeared, like props on a stage, for the figures to sit on or under. Toward the end of the Tang dynasty, mountain and river landscapes began to come into prominence (the Chinese term for landscape painting is *san shui*, literally translated, "mountains water"). The human figure, when seen at all, whether alone or in groups, is dwarfed. Similarly the presence of manmade structures is minimal.

The Tang poet-painter Wang Wei (701–761) is considered the genius who inaugurated the great tradition of landscape scroll painting—he is sometimes called the Leonardo da Vinci of Chinese painting. We know his work only in copies, the most famous of which is one by the fourteenth-century artist Zhao Mengfu [Chao Meng-fu] (about whom more below), now owned by the British Museum. The lost original, the first of its kind, was a horizontal scroll painting over twenty feet long. This work, and all subsequent landscape paintings in this format, were not meant to be seen all stretched out at once but rather a few feet at a time as the scroll was unrolled and simultaneously rerolled moving from the right end of the scroll to the left. One might consider this an early moving picture. There is no break between scenes, and the land-

Figure 65. In this detail from the Tang-dynasty scroll painting,
Palace Ladies Tuning the Lute and Drinking Tea, *the artist concentrates on the figures and uses landscape elements only as props or compositional dividers.* The Nelson-Atkins Museum of Art, Kansas City, Missouri, Nelson Fund

scape is continuous from end to end, so that the viewer follows a visual narrative from one perfectly composed section to the next, here wandering along a mountain path, there crossing a bridge, stopping at a house where people are having tea, watching a fisherman in his boat on the river, and so on. There is time for solitude among rocks and trees, time for the contemplation of vistas, time to get lost in the mountains beyond mists.

Wang Wei's own brushwork in either calligraphy or painting is lost to us, but his voice can be heard in the following poem, which is surely a painting in words:

Duckweed Pond

By the spring pond, deep and wide,
you must be waiting for the light boat to return.
Supple and soft, the green duckweed meshes,
till dangling willow sweep it open again.[1]

1. Wang Wei in Burton Watson, trans., *The Columbia Book of Chinese Poetry* (New York: Columbia University Press, 1984), 201.

The tradition begun by Wang Wei has fostered hundreds of thousands of landscape scrolls. Artists of every dynasty and era since his time have been celebrated for *their* particular way of handling the brushstrokes and the composition.

Rather than make any attempt here to catalog even the best known of the many styles, schools, and artists of the past thousand years, we will instead look at two samples of thirteenth-century Chinese landscapes, one from the Southern Song dynasty, the other from the Yuan, and contrast them not only with each other but also with a nineteenth-century European engraving of a Chinese mountain and river scene. While the Chinese works are aesthetically superior, the three do share two significant common elements: They are predominantly conceived in black and white, and all have as their subject a Chinese landscape. Once some general notion of the Chinese artists' sensibilities is gained by means of this exercise, it may be easier to trace the immensely intricate differences between the successive generations of Chinese painters and calligraphers of the last thousand years.

In considering the Chinese works, the first step must be to put aside all preconceptions associated with Western artistic traditions and to look carefully at what is conveyed with brush and ink on silk or paper. The Southern Song painting, ink on silk with slight color, is a work of the well-known artist Ma Yuan (active 1190–1225), sometimes called One-corner Ma because of the lopsided composition typical of his works. From a balustrade, a scholar, attended by another figure, observes the grandeur of a waterfall and gorge. Two trees, clearly distinguishable by the calligraphic strokes that describe their foliage, and a foreground rock dominate the composition. We cannot tell if the sun is shining, if shadows are being cast. There are dark and light sides to the tree trunk, but this could be read as dark moss growing on the damper side rather than the shadowing of a sunlit scene. In the original, the subdued tones of the color washes are scarcely distinguishable from the black ink tones, and they are not missed as we look at the black and white reproduction. Ultimately, when we have considered all the elements of the picture, we return to the man and wonder what passes through his mind as he contemplates the

傑日為小學書之餘時々戲弄小筆杜
松山水稻不能工蓋自唐以来如王右丞大李
將軍鄭虔盧文通石奇絕々此不能一二見盖五
代苦湖董元輩出尤与少此筆意連綿
傑而作者維未散与古人此絕視之此畫手則
自謂少墨可回野雲家書故土其未為湖

Figure 66. At left, the famous Southern Song artist Ma Yuan painted this album leaf, Scholar by a Waterfall, *in ink and light color on silk.* The Metropolitan Museum of Art, gift of the Dillon Fund, 1973

Figure 67. At top, Chao Mengfu, foremost artist of the Yuan dynasty, used ink on paper for this hand scroll, Twin Pines against a Flat Vista. *The Metropolitan Museum of Art, gift of the Dillon Fund, 1973*

Figure 68. Above, The Hea Hills *is a French nineteenth-century engraving.* New York Public Library Picture Collection

roaring brook that bubbles between the rocks in the lower right-hand corner of the picture.

In the second Chinese work, done in ink on paper, the renowned Yuan dynasty painter Zhao Mengfu (1254–1322), has quite turned the case around. The human presence, barely seen, of the tiny fisherman in his boat seems only a compositional element to let us know that we are looking at vast distances between foreground, middleground, and background. He also serves a narrative purpose by telling us that the empty space that occupies most of the lower half of the composition is water and that the landscape is not a total wilderness. The expressive calligraphic strokes of the pine trees and rocks of the foreground are brilliantly individual in a way that makes the pine tree in Ma Yuan's work appear, by comparison, as a highly skilled but conceivably repeatable exercise. The same is true of the mountains and shorthand notations indicating trees in the distance. Once again, the dark washes on the underside of the rocks indicate form more than shadow, and function primarily as compositional ballast to the sweeping areas of emptiness. We let our eye rove back and forth across this scene until we feel we are looking directly at a place that may not even exist beyond this scroll but that allows us to enter its grand space directly, without the intermediary of an observer within the painting. We do not identify with the fisherman, who is concentrating on catching a fish and whose vantage point in any case could not provide a better composition than the one before us. In Zhao Mengfu's painting, we are the only viewer, and the painting itself replaces nature as the object of contemplation. We admire more the way it has been done than the real view or phenomena it may represent. The calligraphy of the strokes matter more than the subject.

To the connoisseur, the differences between the two Chinese paintings described above are enormous. To the untrained Western eye, they seem hardly worth mentioning. And if we contrast them both with the French etching, the paintings suddenly become as akin as peas in a pod. The etching, engraved by one man from a drawing by another (both obscure artists), is clearly a workmanlike illustration of a real place, without the stature of a great artistic achievement, but withal, it fits into the mainstream tradition of

186

European landscape painting. We are in a world where carefully calculated perspective must be consistent throughout the composition. We can tell that the light is coming from the right-hand side of the scene. Water reflects, shadows are cast, the weather report might be told by the clouds in the sky. People are little more than stick figures providing scale to the boats and buildings. The presence of the missionaries is indicated by the church steeples on the left, which look as though they had been transplanted from some Swiss village. No particular human presence conveys mood, and most striking of all, there is no area large or small that has not been covered with a myriad of tiny pen marks, not one of which is remotely interesting in and of itself or related to calligraphy. The European artist is intent on the documentation of physical, geographic, and social reality. This is what Chinese rivers and mountains in this area look like, he seems to be saying, and the river is a useful transportation route for boat traffic; human habitation stays close to the banks because life in these steep mountains is difficult and isolating.

Aside from the subject of mountains and water, the European etching has nothing at all in common with the two Chinese works. The perspective, the attention to light and shadow, the attempt at realism are all matters that the Chinese artists shrug off. Instead, they care about the elegance of the brush strokes, the composition of light and dark masses irrespective of natural light and shadow, and an inconsistent perspective determined by how the paper area should be divided up and what the artist considers the important elements in the picture.

Two other differences between Chinese and Western art have to do with the use of color and the inclusion of writing within the picture. European and American paintings are frequently seen as compositions of color as much as of linear or spacial elements. Lifetimes have been spent in the studio, on both sides of the Atlantic, working out the colors, or palettes, of landscape and figure paintings. The Chinese artists, on the other hand, have seen color as a decorative addition. A landscape had to be successful in black and white first and foremost, whether or not watercolor was added.

Chinese paintings often have writing on them. Sometimes this is put there by the artist and is a poem or comment directly related to the subject depicted. Later owners of a scroll frequently added their own comments. When done with discretion, either outside the area of the picture or along its edge, this is not considered as graffiti spoiling the composition. Quite the contrary. The writing is always done in an expert hand, beautiful to look at for its own sake, and the thoughts expressed add to the enjoyment of the picture. This is the ultimate manifestation of the continuum between calligraphy, poetry, and painting. Sometimes, however, a collector adds his comments and the red stamp of his seal in the center of the composition or, worse, on top of the actual brushwork. This is an intrusion. The worst offender was the Qianlong emperor of the Qing dynasty. The paintings that have come down to us from his vast collection all have one or more such seal stamps, invariably in the most central area of the composition.

Song Dynasty

The tradition of great landscape painting begun by Wang Wei was continued by the Northern Song painters of the tenth and eleventh centuries, but a new subject matter was introduced when the gifted but doomed emperor Song Huizong (see chapter 8) began an imperial academy of art. His personal preference for realistic renderings of birds and flowers and his invention of a new "lean gold style" calligraphy, illustrated in figure 35, became fashionable, and after his capture by northern tribes, these subjects were included, with landscapes, in the small album-leaf and fan paintings of Southern Song masters.

One of the more esoteric groups of artists during the thirteenth century was a sect called the Chan Buddhists, monks who emulated the brushwork of their contemporaries but not the style or composition. The famous painting of six persimmons by Mu Qi [Mu Ch'i] (active in 1269) is an example of their work. There is no setting, no human presence: All we see is the rather two-dimensional silhouettes of six flattened spheres with dark stems and leaves more or less lined up horizontally across the lower half of the page. This style was picked up by Japanese monks visiting their Chinese brethren at the time and brought back to Japan, where it became the basis of the Zen style of Japanese painting and design so celebrated by recent artists and designers in the United States.

Another Song item brought back to Japan by Buddhist monks was the black ceramic tea bowl. This became the prototypical form for the Japanese tea bowls still made and treasured today. It was only one of the Song ceramic forms, however, for this was a time of perfecting the porcelain wares that had first been invented under the Tang. Monochrome glazes of soft jade colors, called celadon in Europe (after the shepherd by that name in a French play who wore a gray-green robe), textured glazes known as hare's fur, and other refined glazing techniques enhanced vases, bowls, and pitchers occasionally adorned with an archaic fish or dragon-motif handles.

Yuan Dynasty

The Mongolian invasion and conquest of the second half of the thirteenth century brought an end to Song refinements. But as we have seen in the painting of that most famous of Yuan dynasty artists, Zhao Mengfu, Chinese art held its own and sought new approaches under the Yuan rule. Politics made some painters flee into seclusion rather than serve the foreign rulers, but Zhao Mengfu was one of the few who accepted the invitation to serve at the court of Kublai Khan in the manner of the classic scholar-official: While copying the works of the Tang master Wang Wei, which he treasured, he was also secretary of the Board of War. Furthermore, his own distinctive style suggested new approaches to landscape painting. His reputation as a painter has long more than compensated for what some have considered his traitorous decision to serve a foreign master.

Zhao Mengfu is also known for his wonderful paintings of animals, especially horses. With the Mongol conquest came a renewed interest in riding and hunting. Mongolian horses were a different breed from the steeds of Tang Taizong, and Zhao Mengfu made the most of their sturdy, powerful proportions. He established a dynasty of artists: His son, grandson, and grandnephew all became celebrated painters of the Yuan era, and at least two of them continued to feature horses in their works.

The Mongolian influence was also evident in the ceramics of the Yuan era, in which the traditional Chinese motifs of dragons and fish mingle with the birds and animals prized by the nomadic hunter. The technique of layering glazes, known as underglazing, proved especially successful with blue on blue, foreshadowing the much-sought-after blue and white ware exported from the Ming dynasty on.

Ming Dynasty

In 1368 the Chinese reclaimed rule over their empire under the leadership of the ex-Buddhist monk best known as Taizu. He proclaimed the Ming dynasty, which lasted until 1644. Since the Ming name is most frequently associated with ceramics in Western minds, especially with blue and white wares, it should be pointed out that the Dutch ware known as delft and the famous willow pattern wares in England both had their origin in Ming designs. The willow pattern was inspired by the traditional Chinese story of two lovers who escaped from disapproving parents to die together on an island reached by a bridge. Their souls became two doves that flew off over a willow tree, freed from parental and worldly constraints. This pattern has become such common tea-shop tableware all over the Western Hemisphere that one rarely stops to recall its origins in the legends of the Ming dynasty.

Brilliant red and yellow monochrome glazes were perfected during the Ming period. Bowls in Ming yellow, the imperial color, were a prize that collectors later killed for.

Perhaps in reaction against these monochrome pieces, a new taste developed in the later fifteenth and early sixteenth centuries for highly decorated ceramics painted with bright enamel glazes. Traditional dragons, peonies, birds, fish, and foliage fill up the surfaces of the pots, bowls, and plates they adorn and remind us that the sensibilities of the Ming had moved far away from the pure, muted colors of the Song.

Figure 69. This blue and white dish, nine inches in diameter, was made for export during Ming dynasty. Private collection

The lure of the ornate did not affect the calligraphers and painters of the Ming period. On the contrary, with the exception of the works of a few great masters who consciously developed their individualist styles, the Ming scrolls show landscapes that are increasingly conservative renditions of the mountain and river scenes favored in the Tang and Song eras. In large part, this was due to the court control of a new school of "professional" painters who painted to order for the imperial household. When "old master" landscapes were not requested, it was genre scenes of riverbanks, domesticated fowl, children, and pets. Treatises on how to paint rocks, trees, and leaves in the style of Wang Wei were studiously followed. Rare was the brush that broke free of this backward-glancing mentality.

Qing Dynasty and the Twentieth Century

By the time the empire was once again brought under foreign rule, this time by the Manchu, in 1644, conservatism had become so entrenched that, until the mid-twentieth century, the master painters of the era were even more reluctant to depart from the traditions than their Ming predecessors. Jesuit artists, trained in Italy, came to live at the Qing court and influenced the official painters. The modeling of the faces in the portraits in this book by Yao Wenhan (figures 2, 4, 8, 10, 20, 25, 27, 32, 34, 37, 39, 40, and 46), most of which are necessarily based on traditional likenesses rather than live subjects, betrays the artist's exposure to Western artistic techniques. Articles produced in factories catered to the taste of the Manchu court, which favored more color, more ornament, and larger size. The great palace-building sprees of the Qing dynasty emperors required huge quantities of decorative objects made by virtual slave laborers in factories all over China. Multicolored floral designs or genre scenes covered porcelain tableware; intricate cloisonné patterns enhanced enameled copperware; jade sculptures were bigger and more elaborate than ever.

What wasn't taken by the imperial households found its way into the export trade and ended up in European and American parlors, where such *chinoiserie* fit perfectly into the ornate, cluttered look of Victorian and Second Empire decors.

An appreciation of Chinese symbolism is important in looking at these artifacts: The dragon is the emperor, the phoenix, the empress; the tortoise symbolizes north and winter, the dragon, east and spring; the bird is south and summer, while the tiger is west and autumn. Plum, pine, and bamboo are the three great friends who stand respectively for Daoism, Buddhism, and Confucianism. The list of Chinese symbols is endless, but it helps to know they exist when considering the decorative subject matter of Qing art.

For those interested in the dating of Qing artifacts, the following table may be handy. In dating these artifacts, museums and antique shops use the reign name of the emperor under whom they were made.

Reign Name	*Dates*
Kangxi [K'ang-hsi] ("Lasting Peace")	1661–1722
Yongzheng [Yung-cheng] ("Kind and Proper")	1722–1735
Qianlong [Ch'ien-lung] ("Heavenly and Grand")	1735–1796
Jiaqing [Chia-ch'ing] ("Fine Celebration")	1796–1820

Daoguang [Tao-kuang] ("Road of Glory")	1820–1850
Xianfeng [Hsien-feng] ("Complete Bumper Crop")	1850–1861
Tongzhi [T'ung-chih] ("Govern Together")	1861–1875
Guangxu [Kuang-hsu] ("Connecting Glory")	1875–1908

Fortunately for museum-goers, the masterpieces of earlier dynastic eras were recognized and collected by some discerning "foreign devils" whose personal acquisitions have helped to form the great Oriental art collections of Western museums. But because many of these works were plundered in the nineteenth century from sites without benefit of archeological identification, their context and cultural significance was lost until recent scholarship began to establish their place in art history. The rise of archeological activity in China in the last sixty years has provided much needed data on everything from Shang bronzes to Tang pottery figures, and today we are uniquely in a position to appreciate the rich cultural heritage in these museum displays.

In the twentieth century, two world wars and the Chinese revolution have prevented significant contact between East and West. We in the West have been out of touch with Chinese art, and they with ours. Since 1949, Chinese art has to a great extent been enrolled in the service of revolutionary propaganda. There have been a handful of persistent individuals who have painted as they chose or not at all. In their work, the calligraphic tradition is sometimes combined with the Western media of oil and acrylic on canvas or paper. Young artists who lived through the Cultural Revolution, when many of China's great cultural monuments were desecrated by the Red Guards, are reacknowledging their heritage. Some have been influenced by visiting the Buddhist cave shrines. The murals of Dunhuang, in particular, have been a point of departure for explorations of figure painting and color abstraction. Others have found inspiration in the colorful traditions of minority peoples. One waits with curiosity to see what these talented pioneers will make of their long and varied past.

APPENDIX III

PLACES TO VISIT

T he following is a listing of text references to places of historical interest which may be on the traveler's itinerary. Consult the index for references in the text.

Anyang [An-yang], Henan [Ho-nan] province (Shang capital)
Beijing [Peking]
    Great Wall at Badaling, north of Beijing
    Marco Polo Bridge, 10 miles southwest of Beijing
    Museum of National History
    Palace Museum (Forbidden City)
Changsha [Ch'ang-sha], Hunan province, Mawangdui tombs
Chongqing [Chung-ch'ing, Chungking], Sichuan [Ssu-ch'uan] province (point of embarcation for Yangtse cruises)
Dangtu [Tang-t'u], Anhui [An-hui, Anhwei] province, Li Bai's tomb (hard to reach)
Datong, Shanxi [Shan-hsi, Shansi] province, Yungang [Yun-kang] Caves (Buddhist shrine)
Dunhuang [Tun-huang], Gansu [Kan-su] province, Mogao [Mo-kao] Grottoes (Buddhist shrine)

Hangzhou [Hang-chou], Zhejiang [Che-chiang, Chekiang] province (Song dynasty capital)

Jiaxiang [Chia-hsiang], Shandong [Shan-tung] province, Wu family tombs (Han dynasty reliefs)

Luoyang [Lo-yang], Henan [Ho-nan] province, Longmen [Lungmen] Caves (Buddhist shrine)

Qufu [Chü-fu], Shandong [Shan-tung] province, Confucius's place of birth and death

Tai Shan, Shandong [Shan-tung] province, sacred Daoist mountain

Xi'an [Hsi-an], Shaanxi [Shen-hsi, Shensi] province

    Banpo [Pan-p'o], Neolithic site

    Chang'an, Han and Tang capital

    Great Goose Pagoda, Tang pagoda

    Hao, Western Zhou capital

    Shaanxi [Shen-hsi, Shensi] Provincial Museum

    Tomb army of Qin Shihuangdi

    Xianyang [Hsien-yang], Qin capital

Yan'an, Shaanxi [Shen-hsi, Shensi] province, cave homes of Mao and followers, 1935–49

Zhaozhou [Chao-chou] Bridge, Hebei [Ho-pei] province, sixth-century Sui bridge (hard to get to)

RECOMMENDED
READING LIST

The titles below, while they represent only a fragment of the literature on China available in English, are selected as useful starting points for the general reader who wishes to explore further. In some cases, the books will be available only in libraries or secondhand editions. However, as either the best of their kind or, as in the case of the Legge translations, the most complete, they are worth hunting for.

General History

Fairbank, John K., Edwin O. Reischauer, and Albert M. Craig. *East Asia, Tradition and Transformation*. Boston: Houghton Mifflin Company, 1978.

Gernet, Jacques. *A History of Chinese Civilization*. Cambridge: Cambridge University Press, 1985.

Hucker, Charles O. *China's Imperial Past*. Palo Alto, Calif.: Stanford University Press, 1975.

Latourette, Kenneth Scott. *The Chinese, Their History and Culture*. New York: Macmillan, 1972.

Ancient History and Archeology

Chang, K. C. *Art, Myth and Ritual.* Cambridge, Mass.: Harvard University Press, 1983.

Hirth, Friedrich. *The Ancient History of China.* Freeport, N.Y.: Books For Libraries Press, 1969.

Keightley, David N., ed. *Origins of Chinese Civilization.* Berkeley: University of California Press, 1983.

Qin Dynasty (221–207 B.C.)

Cotterell, Arthur. *The First Emperor of China.* New York: Holt, Rinehart and Winston, 1981.

Han Dynasty (206 B.C.–A.D. 220)

Szuma Chien (Sima Qian). *Selections from Records of the Historian.* Translated by Yang Hsien-yi and Gladys Yang. Beijing: Foreign Languages Press, 1979.

Three Kingdoms

See below under Literature.

Sui Dynasty (581–618)

Wright, Arthur. *The Sui Dynasty.* New York: Alfred A. Knopf, 1979.

Tang Dynasty (618–907)

Wright, Arthur, and Dennis Twitcett, eds. *Perspectives on the T'ang.* New Haven: Yale University Press, 1973.

See also van Gulik under Literature.

Song Dynasty (960–1279)

Gernet, Jacques. *Daily Life in China on the Eve of the Mongol Invasion 1250–1276.* New York: Macmillan, 1962.

Yuan (Mongol) Dynasty (1271–1368)

Ronald Latham, trans. *The Travels of Marco Polo*. Harmondsworth, Eng.: Penguin Books, 1982.

Ming Dynasty (1368–1644)

Dreyer, Edward L. *Early Ming China*. Palo Alto, Calif.: Stanford University Press, 1982.

Huang, Ray. *1587, A Year of No Significance*. New Haven: Yale University Press, 1981.

Qing Dynasty (1644–1911)

Smith, Richard. *China's Cultural Heritage: The Ch'ing Dynasty, 1644–1912*. Boulder, Colo.: The Westview Press, 1983.

Spence, Jonathan. *The Death of Woman Wang*. Harmondsworth, Eng.: Penguin Books, 1985.

Warner, Marina. *The Dragon Empress: Life and Times of Tz'u Hsi 1835–1908, Empress Dowager of China*. New York: Macmillan, 1982.

Twentieth Century

Butterfield, Fox. *China, Alive in the Bitter Sea*. New York: Bantam Books, 1983.

Clubb, Edmund O. *20th Century China*. New York: Columbia University Press, 1978.

Fairbank, John King. *Chinabound: A Memoir*. New York: Harper Colophon Books, 1982.

Heng, Liang, and Judith Shapiro. *Son of the Revolution*. New York: Vintage Books, 1984.

Mathews, Jay and Linda. *One Billion*. New York: Ballantine Books, 1985.

Salisbury, Harrison. *China, 100 Years of Revolution*. London: Andre Deutsch, 1983.

Snow, Edgar. *Red Star over China*. New York: Bantam Books, 1984.

Spence, Jonathan. *The Gate of Heavenly Peace: The Chinese and Their Revolution, 1895–1980*. Harmondsworth, Eng.: Penguin Books, 1982.

Literature

Cao Xueqin. *The Story of the Stone.* 2 vols. Translated by David Hawkes. Harmondsworth, Eng.: Penguin Books, 1977. Published also as *Dream of the Red Chamber, see* Tsao Hsüeh-chin.

Dillard, Annie. *Encounters with Chinese Writers.* Middletown, Conn.: Wesleyan University Press, 1984.

Liu, Wu-chi, and Irving Lo, eds. *Sunflower Splendor: Three Thousand Years of Chinese Poetry.* New York: Doubleday Anchor Books, 1975.

Liu, Wu-chi. *An Introduction to Chinese Literature.* Bloomington, Ind.: Indiana University Press, 1966.

Lo Kuan-chung. *Three Kingdoms.* Translated by Moss Roberts. New York: Pantheon Books, 1976.

Lu Xun. *Selected Works.* Translated by Yang Xianyi and Gladys Yang. Beijing: Foreign Languages Press, 1980.

Owen, Stephen. *The Great Age of Chinese Poetry: The High Tang.* New Haven: Yale University Press, 1981.

Tsao Hsüeh-chin. *Dream of the Red Chamber.* Translated by Wang Chi-chen. New York: Doubleday Anchor Books, 1958.

van Gulik, Robert. *The Chinese Gold Murders* and others in the Judge Dee mystery series, set in the Tang dynasty. Chicago: University of Chicago Press, 1979.

Watson, Burton. *The Columbia Book of Chinese Poetry.* New York: Columbia University Press, 1984.

Wu Ch'eng-en (Wu Chengen). *Monkey: Folk Novel of China.* Translated by Arthur Waley. New York: Grove Press, 1958. Published also as *Journey to the West.* 4 vols. Translated by Anthony C. Yu. Chicago: University of Chicago Press, 1983.

Art

Cahill, James. *Chinese Painting.* New York: Rizzoli International Publications, 1985.

Hopkirk, Peter. *Foreign Devils on the Silk Road.* Amherst: University of Massachusetts Press, 1984.

Lee, Sherman. *A History of Far Eastern Art.* New York: Prentice-Hall and Harry N. Abrams, 1973.

Sato, Masahiko. *Chinese Ceramics: A Short History*. New York and Tokyo: Weatherhill/Heibonsha, 1981.

Sullivan, Michael. *The Arts of China*. Berkeley: University of California Press, 1984.

Tregear, Mary. *Chinese Art*. Oxford: Oxford University Press, 1980.

Watson, William. *Style in the Arts of China*. Harmondsworth, Eng.: Penguin Books, 1974.

Weng, Wan-go. *Chinese Painting and Calligraphy*. New York: Dover Publications, 1978.

Philosophy and Religion

deBary, Theodore et al. *Sources of Chinese Tradition*. New York: Columbia University Press, 1960.

Fung Yu-lan. *A History of Chinese Philosophy*. Translated by Derk Bodde. Princeton: Princeton University Press, 1952.

Legge, James, trans. *The Chinese Classics*. 7 vols. Oxford: Clarendon Press, 1872–1895. Reprint. Hong Kong: Hong Kong University Press, 1954.

Legge, James, trans. *The Texts of Taoism*. 2 vols. New York: Dover Publications, 1962. Some of Legge's translations have been reissued by Dover Publications and the Paragon Book Reprint Corp. Other, more up-to-date translations of some of the Chinese classics are also available, most notably D. C. Lau, trans., *Confucius: The Analects*, Harmondsworth, Eng.: Penguin Books, 1970.

Wright, Arthur F. *Buddhism in Chinese History*. Palo Alto, Calif.: Stanford University Press, 1974.

Wright, Arthur F., ed. *Confucianism and Chinese Civilization*. Palo Alto, Calif.: Stanford University Press, 1975.

Science and Technology

Needham, Joseph. *Science in Traditional China*. Cambridge, Mass.: Harvard University Press, 1982.

Needham, Joseph. *The Shorter Science and Civilization in China*. 2 vols. Edited by C. Ronan. Cambridge: Cambridge University Press, 1981.

Travel

Kaplan, Frederic, and Arne de Keijzer. *The China Guidebook*. New York: Eurasia Press, 1986.

Samagalski, A., and M. Buckley. *China: A Travel Survival Kit*. Victoria, Australia: Lonely Planet Publications, 1984.

Schwartz, Brian. *China Off the Beaten Track*. New York: St. Martin's Press, 1983.

Theroux, Paul. *Sailing through China*. Boston: Houghton Mifflin Company, 1984.

INDEX

Main entries for Chinese names, locations, and terms mentioned in this book are generally indexed under their pinyin romanization. Unless otherwise indicated, these entries list the pinyin form first, followed by the Wade-Giles form in brackets and any conventional or alternate spelling in parentheses. Please note exceptions to pinyin romanization in the Guide to Spelling, Pronunciation, and Dates.